The Transformation and Declir

Studies in European History Series

Series Editors: Julian Jackson
                                   Peter Wilson
                                   Sarah Badcock

Catherine Baker   *The Yugoslav Wars of the 1990s*
Jeremy Black   *A Military Revolution? Military Change and European
                         Society, 1550–1800*
T.C.W. Blanning   *The French Revolution: Class War or Culture Clash?* (2nd edn)
John Breuilly   *The Formation of the First German Nation-State, 1800–1871*
Peter Burke   *The Renaissance* (2nd edn)
Markus Cerman   *Villagers and Lords in Eastern Europe, 1300–1800*
Michael L. Dockrill &
Michael F. Hopkins   *The Cold War 1945–1991* (2nd edn)
William Doyle   *The Ancien Régime* (2nd edn)
William Doyle   *Jansenism*
Andy Durgan   *The Spanish Civil War*
Geoffrey Ellis   *The Napoleonic Empire* (2nd edn)
Donald A. Filtzer   *The Krushchev Era*
Karin Friedrich   *Brandenburg-Prussia, 1466–1806*
Mary Fulbrook   *Interpretations of the Two Germanies, 1945–1990* (2nd edn)
Graeme Gill   *Stalinism* (2nd edn)
Hugh Gough   *The Terror in the French Revolution* (2nd edn)
Peter Grieder   *The German Democratic Republic*
John Henry   *The Scientific Revolution and the Origins of Modern Science*
                         (3rd edn)
Stefan-Ludwig
Hoffmann   *Civil Society, 1750–1914*
Beat Kümin   *The Communal Age in Western Europe, c.1100–1800*
Henry Kamen   *Golden Age Spain* (2nd edn)
Richard Mackenney   *The City-State, 1500–1700*
Spencer Mawby   *The Transformation and Decline of the British Empire*
Andrew Porter   *European Imperialism, 1860–1914*
Roy Porter   *The Enlightenment* (2nd edn)
Roger Price   *The Revolutions of 1848*
James Retallack   *Germany in the Age of Kaiser Wilhelm II*
Richard Sakwa   *Communism in Russia*
Geoffrey Scarre &   *Witchcraft and Magic in 16th- and 17th-Century Europe*
John Callow   (2nd edn)
R.W. Scribner &
C. Scott Dixon   *The German Reformation* (2nd edn)
Robert Service   *The Russian Revolution, 1900–1927* (4th edn)
Jeremy Smith   *The Fall of Soviet Communism, 1985–1991*
David Stevenson   *The Outbreak of the First World War*
Peter H. Wilson   *The Holy Roman Empire, 1495–1806* (2nd edn)
Oliver Zimmer   *Nationalism in Europe, 1890–1940*

Studies in European History
Series Standing Order ISBN 978–0–333–79365–7
(outside North America only)

You can receive future titles in this series as they are published by placing a standing
order. Please contact your bookseller or, in case of difficulty, write to us at the address
below with your name and address, the title of the series and the ISBN quoted above.

Customer Services Department, Macmillan Distribution Ltd,
Houndmills, Basingstoke, Hampshire, RG21 6XS, UK

The Transformation and Decline of the British Empire

Decolonisation After the First World War

Spencer Mawby

First published 2015 by
PALGRAVE

Palgrave in the UK is an imprint of Macmillan Publishers Limited, registered in England, company number 785998, of 4 Crinan Street, London, N1 9XW.

Palgrave Macmillan in the US is a division of St Martin's Press LLC, 175 Fifth Avenue, New York, NY 10010.

Palgrave is a global imprint of the above companies and is represented throughout the world.

Palgrave® and Macmillan® are registered trademarks in the United States, the United Kingdom, Europe and other countries.

ISBN 978–1–137–38750–9 paperback

This book is printed on paper suitable for recycling and made from fully managed and sustained forest sources. Logging, pulping and manufacturing processes are expected to conform to the environmental regulations of the country of origin.

A catalogue record for this book is available from the British Library.

A catalog record for this book is available from the Library of Congress.

Printed and bound by CPI Group (UK) Ltd, Croydon, CR0 4YY

Contents

Contents

Editors' Preface

The Studies in European History series offers a guide to developments in a field of history that has become increasingly specialized with the sheer volume of new research and literature now produced. Each book has three main objectives. The primary purpose is to offer an informed assessment of opinion on a key episode or theme in European history. Secondly, each title presents a distinct interpretation and conclusions from someone who is closely involved with current debates in the field. Thirdly, it provides students and teachers with a succinct introduction to the topic, with the essential information necessary to understand it and the literature being discussed. Equipped with an annotated bibliography and other aids to study, each book provides an ideal starting point from which to explore important events and processes that have shaped Europe's history to the present day.

Books in the series introduce students to historical approaches which in some cases are very new and which, in the normal course of things, would take many years to filter down to textbooks. By presenting history's cutting edge, we hope that the series will demonstrate some of the excitement that historians, like scientists, feel as they work on the frontiers of their subjects. The series also has an important contribution to make in publicizing what historians are doing, and making it accessible to students and scholars in this and related disciplines.

Julian Jackson
Peter H. Wilson
Sarah Badcock

Acknowledgements

As I begin writing these acknowledgements it is almost exactly two years since the idea for this book was first suggested to me by my colleague Sarah Badcock, who is also one of the editors of this series. What follows would therefore never have been written without her encouragement to tackle the historiography on the end of the British Empire. Old and new comrades in the Department of History at the University of Nottingham have, as always, provided a collegiate environment in which to juggle the conflicting demands on academic staff at a time when collegiality is at a premium in Higher Education.

The book is primarily intended for use by students who, at the behest of government ministers and university administrators, increasingly regard themselves as consumers. Despite these countervailing trends I still like to think of undergraduates as active members of an academic community and the principal aim of this exercise is to encourage its readers to participate in debates about Britain's imperial past. The potential to do this is illustrated in chapter 3 where I used dissertations by two History finalists at the University of Nottingham as a jumping off point for some discussion of events in Uganda and Diego Garcia. In that regard I am greatly obliged to Matt Gainsford and Elizabeth Middleton for demonstrating the kind of initiative and engagement which is still thankfully common among the students whom I teach.

The pace of change often appears swifter in publishing than in academia and the speed with which Palgrave have expedited the publication of this book has been vital in preventing its contents from becoming stale. I am therefore extremely grateful to Sonya Barker and Felicity Noble for taking on this project and then to Rachel Bridgewater for seeing it through to completion, as well as to Praveen Gajamoorthy and his proof reading team for driving on through the editing phase with such expedition.

Lastly back in my old stomping ground of Gateshead thanks are due to Bryan White for his speedy and diligent proof reading and Sheila Mawby for her good advice and consistent encouragement.

Introduction

Everybody knows that the British Empire no longer exists but
nobody is quite certain when it ended. One of the many difficulties with identifying a precise date or period for the 'fall' of the
empire is that its years of decline were also years of dramatic transformation in the politics and society of both metropolitan Britain
and the overseas territories that the British had once governed in
the imperial periphery. The independence ceremonies of newly
liberated countries are perhaps the most conspicuous markers
of national reassertion and imperial decline; but long before the
British abandoned formal political control of their Asian, African
and American colonies, relations between metropolis and periphery were undergoing very significant changes which ramified well
beyond the confines of politics. And even after all were agreed
that the formal British empire was no more, its influence was still
strongly felt in the former colonial territories, in Britain itself and
in the international system.

This book is less concerned with debates between historians
about periodization and more with what they have made of the
dramatic changes which occurred during the era of late British
imperialism. In this vein, what it offers is an introduction to the
very rich literature which has emerged in the last quarter of a century about the nature and character of the British Empire after
1918. Although other starting points could have been adopted, the
four or five decades after the First World War are clearly those
of late imperialism, during which the imperial system was being
transformed into something else. For example, one conspicuous
change was the shift from a political system in which London was
able to exert political control over much of the rest of the world
through a whole variety of constitutional mechanisms to one in
which constitutional authority had been devolved to numerous

1

different centres across Africa, Asia and the Americas. To put it more straightforwardly an imperial world was replaced by a world of nation states. This political shift was accompanied by a series of other developments to which it was related in complex and often indirect ways and which resonate into the present. It is the nature of these transformations and their association with imperial decline which have preoccupied historians in recent years. What this introduction and the following chapters will offer is a summary of what historians have made of these developments, including those questions on which a measure of consensus has emerged and the issues on which they still disagree. In order to start filling the notion of 'transformation' with historiographical content we need to turn to the specific subjects which have particularly concerned historians of late British imperialism. After sketching a general outline of this subject matter, this introductory discussion will turn to more formal questions concerning the methods historians currently use in pursuing their investigations, before concluding with some comments about the scope and idiosyncrasies of the project.

Subject matter

The migration of people from the periphery to the metropolis immediately springs to mind when thinking about the legacy of empire; yet political dependence and independence were not the key variables in deciding who came to Britain and when. For example, most Caribbean migrants arrived during the 15 years before Jamaican and Trinidadian independence in 1962. In that same year Uganda also freed itself from imperial control but it was a decade later, in 1972, that Asian refugees from that country resettled in Britain after they were expelled by Idi Amin's government. The obverse to the arrival in the metropolis of civilians from the empire was the continuing presence of British soldiers, sailors and airmen in what were purported to be newly liberated territories. British and Commonwealth forces participated in the Malayan war until 1960, three years after independence, while one of the first events in the political history of an 'independent' Kuwait was the despatch of British troops to the emirate in 1961 to counter a supposed threat of Iraqi invasion. They returned

Introduction

again in 1990 and 2003 and their status then as junior partners in American-led invasions of Iraq illustrated Britain's reduced status and prestige. Less conspicuous and consequently less well known has been the ongoing influence of the British intelligence services in the newly independent countries of the former British Empire. The question of how the historiography has dealt with these continuities and discontinuities is one of the features of this book. Migration will be tackled in more detail in Chapter 3, while military and intelligence aspects are investigated in Chapter 4.

Notions of imperial legacy are tied to another theme, the vitality of late imperialism. The image of a carefully plotted and orderly retreat from empire orchestrated by jaded Whitehall mandarins and pragmatic British politicians has always been vulnerable to criticism, but over the last quarter of a century it has become wholly unsustainable because of two developments in the secondary literature. In the first of these, analysts of official policy have found that, while British policymakers sometimes recognised the inevitability of a smaller world role, they adapted by finding new ways in which influence could be exerted, ranging from revised penal laws and the extension of police powers to suppress anti-colonial dissent to the use of propaganda, and what now might be called the 'soft power' of culture, to cultivate alliances. As William Roger Louis and Ronald Robinson pointed out in a famous article on the 'Imperialism of Decolonization' published in 1994, in order to retain influence a late burst of activity was undertaken on behalf of the imperial state [12]. Since that decisive intervention, much of the historiography on the diplomacy of British decolonisation emphasises the robust self-assertion of policymaking during the period, as well as the occasionally self-defeating consequences of this dynamism.

A brief sampling of some of this work gives a sense of the wide geographical application of these ideas: Barbara Bush's survey of inter-war Africa found that the forceful reaction of imperial agents to the emergence of anti-colonialism became manifest in various new coercive measures designed to sustain a British presence in the long term [19]; even when the last days of imperialism were upon them, as in India during 1947, Lucy P. Chester discovered that British policymakers adopted innovative strategies to divert the current of political affairs and thereby achieve a

3

settlement to the Indo-Pakistani frontier question which accommodated their postcolonial interests [21]; Christopher Bayly and Tim Harper emphasised the continuing coercive power of the British in Southeast Asia after 1945, which was evident from the often forgotten history of military interventions to regain control of Burma and Malaya after the Second World War [17]; Simon Smith's historiographical survey of the Middle East demonstrated that, even after the Suez catastrophe, the British spurned the notion of becoming a regional lapdog of the United States in favour of their own independent diplomatic line [30]; and, lastly, my own work on the constitutional evolution of the Caribbean suggested that the British jealously hoarded their regional privileges and left the final decision to grant independence until the last possible moment [26].

After this slightly breathless rendering of some examples of British activism taken from the literature on official policy, a consideration of the second development in the historiography requires a move away from a focus on the imperial state and its representatives. Over the last couple of decades the literature on decolonisation has placed greater emphasis on the significance of global historical processes which took place outside the purview, or at least the control, of Whitehall departments and colonial governors. Although there are substantial differences between their approaches, political, economic and cultural historians are increasingly united in their view that earlier generations of historians accorded too much respect to the integrity of national and imperial frontiers. Calls for a globalised history of empire do not come just from radical critics of established historical methodology who wish to 'decentre' or 'provincialise' imperial history, such as Antoinette Burton and Dipesh Chakrabarty, but also from traditional historians, interested in the impact of the self-governing dominions and independent territories on the process of decolonisation, such as John Darwin and A. G. Hopkins [2; 3; 5; 8]. The notion of replacing 'national' histories of empire with a new, transnational history of empires requires historians to embrace subjects such as the global transmission of anti-colonial ideas, the movement of capital and labour across frontiers and even apparently more parochial issues, such as changing concepts of Britishness. It may be useful to consider briefly the way in which these topics lend themselves to the transnational perspective.

The activities of anti-colonial activists across Africa, Asia and the Americas have featured prominently in most studies of the end of the European empires. In recent years, however, much greater emphasis has been given to the fact that almost all of the key figures in this movement, including Marcus Garvey, Kwame Nkrumah, Mohandas Gandhi and Abdullah al-Afghani lived peripatetic lives which entailed the crossing and recrossing of national and imperial frontiers. The facility with which these activists communicated with each other and the circulation of their ideas across continents suggests, for many, that a new globalised history would be better able to account for the phenomenon of anti-colonialism than traditional histories of nations and empires. This impetus towards transnational history has also left its mark on historians of business and empire. The ultimately futile attempt by empires and states to constrain the movement of capital demonstrates just how porous the imperial frontier could be. In the case of the British Empire this led to the establishment during the inter-war period of a strictly regulated sterling area which was intended to sustain the financial influence of the City of London after the political empire had dissolved but which perished shortly afterwards. Alongside the slippery operations of capital, the new institutions of the international labour movement also posed a threat to imperial integrity. The penetration of the British Empire by American trade unionists and Soviet-backed labour activists during the Cold War era further illustrated the fragility of the imperial frontier in the era of decolonisation. Cultural identity may appear a more elusive topic than the operations of labour and capital, but the impact of transnational thinking is evident in the increasingly pervasive idea that modern notions of Britishness were not generated at home in the metropolis but that they were at least partly determined by notions of race, ethnicity and gender, gathered as a consequence of the globalisation which went first with empire-building and then imperial dissolution. The first chapter will outline some of the conclusions historians have offered about the character and global impact of anti-colonialism, the second will consider the way in which Britishness has been represented in the literature on imperial decline, alongside a discussion of domestic politics, and the fifth will examine how scholars have interpreted the operations of international finance and the dramatic changes which occurred in labour relations during the final years of empire.

Methodology

Dividing the very large field of British decolonisation into these smaller sub-plots has the advantage of enabling students to investigate specific areas of the historiography in greater detail. The general structure of what follows is designed to move the reader through from an examination of the impact of ideas and ideologies, beginning with anti-colonialism, to what are characterised as material factors, ending with labour and capital, in order to offer a representative sample of different approaches. Aside from the emphasis that some have accorded to the vitality of official policy and that others have placed on the significance of transnational processes, they do not, when synthesised or combined, add up to a general thesis about decolonisation. Given the different intellectual proclivities and interests of different historians this is hardly surprising. However, what can be identified are the common influences which operate on the scholarship as a whole. Historians may disagree about what the answers are to specific questions about the past, such as whether anti-colonial nationalism was inherently authoritarian or how much influence metropolitan financiers exerted over the process of decolonisation, and they might also argue about what kind of questions historians should be investigating, including whether they should focus on the experience of elites or of ordinary people and what the relative significance of culture, society and politics might be. These are debates about matters of substance; but when we turn to matters of form, which relate to the kinds of resources on which historians draw and the problems which they encounter in trying to answer the substantive questions, it is possible to uncover some general features of the historiography. Four formal characteristics can be identified as exerting a particularly strong influence on the literature: when pursuing their work, historians of decolonisation engage in a form of a conversation, take account of present-day concerns, assimilate new evidence and respond to theory.

Engaging in conversation

When comparing ordinary, everyday conversations to the kind of discussions historians conduct about the past, one is most likely to be struck by the differences: while the latter generally occur over an extended period of time in print or in the formal setting of conferences and workshops, the former take place spontaneously and in a colloquial language which seems distant from the rigid demands of historical scholarship. What they share is that they entail an exchange of observations, views and opinions and can range in character from the temperate and consensual to the argumentative and recriminatory. It is this idea that historical conversations can be marked by agreement and cooperation which is worth registering because students are often more alert to controversy and argument than to the process of incremental development by which historians build on the achievements of earlier writers. In the chapters that follow there are plentiful instances of both but the model of conversation as quarrel is often more conspicuous. For example, John Newsinger's challenge to Thomas Mockaitis's argument that the British employed minimum force in their colonial counterinsurgency campaigns is unusual in the sense that the conversation has stretched over two decades but is, in other respects, a model of the heated contests which frequently take place between revisionist and orthodox views [175; 181]. One particularly prominent example of a historical conversation taking the form of an argument between contesting parties occurred when Bernard Porter published *The Absent-Minded Imperialists* in 2004; the book criticised revisionist accounts which suggested that imperialism played a seminal role in shaping British society, politics and culture at home [111]. Having begun the project in combative form, Porter eventually sounded somewhat abashed by the barrage of criticism he received [112].

Although instances of collaboration tend to be overlooked, the idea that history is always a conversation between directly opposed views is misleading. Bill Schwarz's recent book on race and decolonisation is unusually generous in carefully registering the importance of discussions with peers engaged in a similar endeavour, including Wendy Webster and Stephen Howe [114: xii]. The resulting book, *White Man's World*, has had an enthusiastic reception and this illustrates the point that some interventions elicit a broadly consensual response. Similarly, historians reacted positively to Urvashi Butalia's new account of Indian partition, which emphasised the need to incorporate the experience of marginalised groups. As a consequence, a new literature, which moved away from 'top down' political accounts, began to emerge [126]. Whether they present their publications as an outcome of cooperation or contestation, it is important to recognise that historians are not simply working in a silo on their own set of sources but are participating in a wider conversation with a set of peers who are engaged in a similar enterprise, nor are they cut off from the currents and concerns of the present.

Accounting for the present

Presentism is an ugly word which encapsulates an important and inescapable feature of historical scholarship: because history as the study of the past takes place in the present, current concerns intrude into the literature in ways which are sometimes anticipated and sometimes unexpected. To the extent that it offers an antidote to nostalgia and can be insulated from accusations that it introduces a further element of subjectivism into historical writing, presentism is actually a useful feature of historical writing. Whereas nostalgia generates sealed and sterile depictions of historical events and objects by emphasising the discontinuity between the present and the past, by reconnecting the two, presentism offers the possibility of recontextualising the past and demonstrating uniformities as well as disjunctures across time. The obvious criticism of presentism is that it distracts historians from their true task of engaging with the past on its own terms in order to offer an objective historical account. Although if one follows this line of thought, historians' engagement with contemporary issues may be interpreted as unwarranted subjectivism, it ought to be possible for scholars to pay due attention to the kind of commonly recognised standards which might be used either to judge the veracity of certain sources or to assess the plausibility of different arguments about the past, while engaging with the concerns of the present. Many of the broader questions associated with these matters require a degree of philosophical expertise to answer effectively. Those interested in the historiographical issues arising from the literature on British decolonisation will find more certain ground in addressing the various ways in which present-day concerns have influenced debates about the recent past.

In the aftermath of the American invasion of Iraq attention turned to the origins of the Iraqi nation in British imperial history,

Introduction

as embodied in the mandate system established across portions of the Middle East after the First World War. The parallels between the American occupation of the 2000s and the British occupation of the 1920s struck journalists and historians as significant and were anatomised in detail by Toby Dodge. He identified a common pattern in the failed nation-building efforts of the Western powers: first, Western efforts to establish order were frustrated, and then, as a consequence, the occupying forces became increasingly reliant on coercion rather than effective administration to govern the country; lastly, and because of these earlier failures, efforts to inculcate a civic Iraqi identity failed [22]. The commonalities between the periods of British and American occupation are suggestive, right down to the corrosive effect which the Iraq episode had on the credibility of Western governments, but it is rare for historians to find quite such a close match between the past and the present and even in the case of Iraq, care needs to be taken to register discrepancies. The differences between the decentralised Ottoman system of rule, which dissolved after the First World War, and the autocratic and centralising Baathist system, which collapsed under American bombardment 80 years later, were marked, as were the constitutional solutions adopted by the occupying powers. For example, in the 1920s the British attempted to impose a monarchical system, while after 2003 the Americans retained the republican form of government.

The influence of the present is often more evident in the search for continuities with the past than in the attempt to discover precise parallels. In such cases, changes over time are acknowledged, while the continuing relevance of longstanding trends is identified. One highly charged debate which follows this pattern is the question of whether the authoritarianism of many African governments, such as those of Robert Mugabe in Zimbabwe and Teodoro Obiang in Equatorial Guinea, can be traced to the autocratic tendencies of anti-colonial nationalism. It is in this context that the legacy of the Ghanaian, Kwame Nkrumah, who in 1957 became the first nationalist leader in sub-Saharan Africa to secure independence for his country, has become particularly contentious. The long-standing critique of Ali Mazrui has been predicated on the notion that Nkrumah grafted Leninist ideas about the vanguard role of a revolutionary party onto traditional African paternalism to produce an ideological hybrid which

9

permanently damaged the politics of the continent [53: 5–60]. Kwame Botwe-Asamoah has responded to the critique of scholars such as Mazrui with an unstinting endorsement of Nkrumah's record, while Ama Biney recently offered a more qualified defence. On their accounts it was the military coup against Nkrumah in 1966 and the emergence of authoritarian and coercive regimes elsewhere in Africa which were more significant in entrenching African dictatorships [35; 39]. Moving back from the old imperial periphery to British politics, recent fractious arguments about immigration often seem to ignore the role of the imperial legacy in shaping the country's demography. If politicians tend to gloss over this past, historians of immigration have been acutely conscious of the currency and contentiousness of their subject, to the extent that some of the sourness which attends party political debates has infected the historiography. This was particularly evident in Randall Hansen's response to Kathleen Paul's argument that race had always been the key variable in determining the British government's policies on immigration. Hansen was uninhibited in accusing advocates of this racialisation theory, including Paul, of being politically motivated and selective in their use of the archival record [140; 145].

In a slightly less contentious register, the present can provide a context for historical research in the sense that it suggests questions and potential answers. This more indirect route from present to past is evident in Peter Cain and Antony Hopkins's ambitious two-volume history of British imperialism. One of the key arguments of these books was that the management of the empire reflected a British proclivity for 'sound money', represented by the gentlemanly capitalists of the City of London, even at the expense of British manufacturing interests in the north of the country [216; 217]. Such notions had obvious contemporary resonance at a time when the Thatcher government was superintending a policy of deindustrialisation in the old manufacturing regions of Britain alongside financial deregulation of the City. More recently, gathering interest in the role of the Welsh, Irish and Scottish in both the creation and dissolution of the British Empire, as articulated by John MacKenzie in his advocacy of a 'four nations approach' to imperialism, has as its contemporary backdrop the devolution of varying degrees of political power to assemblies in Cardiff, Belfast and Edinburgh [13]. In the aftermath of the close result of the hotly contested referendum on Scottish independence, this four nations conceptualisation of imperial history appears more relevant today than ever before.

Assimilating new evidence

There is a popular perception that historians spend a great deal of their time attempting to uncover documents which have been hidden or suppressed, while the mundane reality is that many of them spend most of their professional lives in well-appointed archives which contain precisely ordered inventories. The British National Archives at Kew is the epitome of this kind of institution and the majority of the books and articles referred to in this book could not have been written without access to the material held there. But this dependency on the official records has its own dangers. Some dramatic discoveries pertaining to decolonisation have revealed the extent to which it is possible for official records to present a sanitised history of events. Twenty years ago historians were unaware of the amount of material which was missing from the official archive. It is now evident that the gaps in the record are much larger than previously suspected. As Edward Hampshire's recent article concerning the incineration of records about the Malayan insurgency of 1948–1960 demonstrates, some of the files have literally gone up in smoke [7]. More pressing because it is unresolved, is the question of the nature of the extant material which is being held at the once secret governmental archive in Hanslope Park. The existence of this collection was only revealed in 2011 as a consequence of judicial intervention in the case of former Mau Mau detainees from Kenya seeking compensation from the British government. Having acknowledged that a significant portion of the documentary record had been withheld, the government authorised a phased release of documents concerning former colonial territories. A further revelation two years later indicated that the archive of 'lost' material was considerably larger than originally estimated. Some preliminary findings from the first batch of newly liberated files have been published, including David Anderson's analysis of the complicity of the Kenyan administration in the application of extreme violence during the Mau Mau war [158]. The chapter on migration in this volume also utilises some new material concerning Diego Garcia, but it will take time for this latest evidence to have an impact on the historiography.

Even before the Hanslope Park disclosure the access regime under which historians operated had changed considerably. The first important development in enabling historians to view previously classified material was the Waldegrave Initiative on Open Government in 1993 which marked a liberalisation in the interpretation of the Public Records Acts of 1958 and 1967. Keith Kyle, a journalist who became the most influential historian of the Suez crisis, immediately conducted an audit of the new material pertaining to the most dramatic event in the post-war history of decolonisation and concluded that it was interesting rather than revelatory; this reflected a general sense that the practical consequences of the initiative for scholars were quite limited [11]. The enactment of the Freedom of Information Bill in 2000, which has been much used by journalists to gain information on contentious current affairs and by ordinary citizens to discover what information public authorities hold about them, also had implications for historians. It offers a more secure basis on which to request material which, on the grounds of its sensitivity, has not been released after the customary 30 year period. Prior to the act it had been possible to challenge such decisions under the old legislation but this gradual liberalisation of the regulations governing access to sensitive material has been particularly useful to historians of intelligence who have also benefitted from a parallel process that has witnessed the erosion of the blanket exemptions previously slapped on intelligence material. Under the restrictions operating 25 years ago it would have been impossible for books such as Rory Cormac's *Confronting the Colonies* or Calder Walton's *Empires of Intelligence* to have offered such a detailed rendition of the operations of the intelligence agencies during the era of decolonisation [189; 210].

New documentary material emerges not just from the efforts of historians, or in the case of Hanslope Park, the judiciary, to loosen the official grip on confidential material, but also from the collection and collation of material by archivists. Some long available, non-governmental records pertinent to the domestic politics of decolonisation have simply been underutilised. Since Stephen Howe employed some of them to write the history of anti-colonialism in British politics, the records of organisations such as the Movement for Colonial Freedom, the Fabian Colonial Bureau, the Africa Bureau and the Union of Democratic Control have been rather neglected [72]. Such institutional records still offer only a partial picture and it has often been more difficult for historians to uncover material of relevance to the experience of the black and Asian population of Britain, particularly during the years prior to the arrival of the *Windrush* in 1948. Despite these impediments, scholars such as Laura Tabili and Hakim Adi have been adept at deploying a variety of public and private sources to analyse the role of migrant workers and students in late imperial Britain [120; 151]. In this context the opening of the Black Cultural Archives in Brixton in 2014 will have a significant impact both in publicising the existence of an extensive range of material pertaining to the precolonial, colonial and postcolonial experience of black people in Britain and in facilitating access to material, such as the papers of Ansel Wong and Jeffrey Green, of interest to scholars of decolonisation. These archives also include an oral history of the Black Women's Movement in Britain, which currently contains testimony from 36 women; this points to the possibility of new documentary material emerging through the recording of people's memories by themselves, by archivists or by historians. Many of those who experienced the effects of the end of the British Empire are still alive and conversations with them provided the basis for Mike and Trevor Phillips's account of the experience of the *Windrush* generation and for Joanna Herbert's writings about the arrival of Ugandan Asians in Britain in 1972 [141; 146].

Responding to theoretical considerations

Although they may be reluctant to engage with large-scale conceptual analysis, the most empirically minded of historians must admit that facts do not speak for themselves: they need to be interpreted. And once questions of interpretation arise, matters of theory inevitably impinge. Even the blandest historical narrative will contain some implicitly theoretical element. For example the chronology at the end of this book could merely have recorded the dates on which newly independent countries were established; had it done so, readers would have been justified in assuming a commitment to the idea, or theory, that these moments were seminal points of transformation. The decision to include later events reflects an alternative theory that there was a substantial measure of continuity after the last remnants of British political control were abandoned. Between the basic practical requirement for some criteria in choosing what to include and what to exclude and the complex and encompassing ideas which underpin the philosophy of history, there are levels of intermediate theorising and it is worth identifying two of these.

The first operates in the regions of small well-defined topics which are often covered in a PhD thesis or a research monograph. When producing this kind of work, the historian is required to revise an existing consensus and, although this might simply be described as rethinking or reorienting, it is probably more accurate to say that a new theory about the past is being offered. Perhaps the most dramatic instance of the explosive implications arising from apparently modest projects has been Caroline Elkins's reinterpretation of British counterinsurgency policy in Kenya. Her project, which was published as *Imperial Reckoning*, began as a dissertation proposal about the significance of the detention camps established during the Mau Mau insurgency, and eventually landed her in the midst of a series of British court hearings, which secured compensation for former Mau Mau detainees and led to the uncovering of a trove of new documentary material about the end of empire [6; 166]. At the other end of the historiographical scale we have more self-conscious attempts to retheorise imperial history as a whole. The work of Cain and Hopkins remains the most conspicuous example of this kind of revisionism from the last quarter of a century. Their arguments had familiar elements, such as the reassertion of the importance of the expansionist tendencies of capital in explaining British encroachment into Africa, Asia and the Americas; but it was the detailed and persuasive account of the emergence and then flourishing of a gentlemanly capitalist class, whose fortunes were intimately tied to empire, which made the two volumes of *British Imperialism* so original and persuasive. They synthesised enormous amounts of quantitative and qualitative evidence into a coherent theory and applied it across nearly three centuries of history. As might be expected from their prioritisation of financial influences on policymaking, in dealing with the 20th century they argued for a degree of continuity into the period of independence on the basis of the large shadow cast by the City of London across the former imperial periphery during an apparently postcolonial era [216; 217].

The case of Cain and Hopkins is also helpful in illustrating the influence of broader intellectual currents on historians because they are part of a tradition of writing about empire, usually associated with the two strikingly different figures of Hobson and Lenin, which emphasises material factors, especially the relationship between capital and labour. This was anomalous to the extent that the era of decolonisation was also the era in which the traditional methodology of the humanities was challenged by theories of structuralism, poststructuralism and postcolonialism. The influence of these revolutionary trends in philosophy has been particularly evident in the so-called new imperial history which has shifted the historiographical centre of gravity from economic considerations towards culture. Any attempt at compressing these ideas into a couple of sentences risks distorting them into unrecognisability but a brief summary is necessary in order to establish their connections to historical scholarship. Structuralism marked a transfer in philosophical interest towards culture, including language, as an instrument for shaping human society and in particular for demarcating different forms of identity. Many of the ideas of the structuralists were continuous with those of the poststructuralists and it is notoriously difficult to place some thinkers in one camp or the other, but the latter can be characterised by their emphasis on the great difficulty, or impossibility, of placing oneself and one's beliefs outside the system of externally imposed cultural norms, in order to make independent, objective judgements. The work of thinkers often identified with poststructuralism, such as Michel Foucault and Julia Kristeva, has been of particular interest to historians of empire. Postcolonialism, in turn, overlaps with poststructuralism but the former is concerned principally with challenging the privileges which the West has accorded itself by identifying the peoples and culture of imperial subjects as different and inferior to those of white European imperialists.

The postcolonial project entails both uncovering the way in which modern Western conceptions of categories such as race and gender were constructed during the process of empire building and offering a new scholarly and political agenda founded on a respect for difference when and where it is located. One can observe the influence of postcolonialism in many different historiographical settings, such as Mithi Mukherjee's reinterpretation of Gandhian ideology, which attempts to unmoor it from the Western practices to which many Western academics have attempted to tie it, Jo Littler's audit of both the imperial presences and absences at the Festival of Britain and Luise White's exploration of the way in which new labour practices generated novel reactions in Africa and, in particular, their connection to an emergent mythology of vampires [56; 107; 257]. What these and many other examples demonstrate is that the attempt to answer very large philosophical questions does percolate downwards to the daily practices of historians.

Conclusions

Finally a word must be added about the limitations and idiosyncrasies of what follows. Needless to say, I have not been able to read every article and book which has been published about the end of the British Empire. Some topics, such as the changes which occurred to imperial cities in the era of decolonisation or the emergence and development of the Commonwealth, have been omitted or mentioned only very briefly. What I have attempted to achieve is fairly broad geographical and chronological coverage, and for those subjects which are covered the texts included are the ones I found interesting, illuminating or provocative; however, such judgements are personal and another historian undertaking the same enterprise would have chosen to discuss different authors. Even those texts which are included in the survey are represented by a précis of what are often quite complex arguments and no doubt some authors may feel that the nuances of their work, or even perhaps its central themes, have not been rendered with sufficient care. If my fellow historians have little in the way of recourse in such cases, students at least are advised to consult the original texts and not depend on the radically abridged iterations offered by this book. One thing which I have tried to avoid in summarising the texts is an overreliance on adjectives to carry the weight of the analysis: the stuff of many book reviews, describing texts as sublime, magisterial or superlative does not take the discussion very far; nor does indicting them as banal, misconceived or fatuous. In that latter regard, tempting as it was, I have avoided including some texts which struck me as relevant but particularly problematic either in their methodology or substantive analysis. In what may be regarded as an act of scholarly hubris I have also chosen to mention my own work and experiences at various points in the text and in doing so I have represented myself in the first person rather than the third. The former risks charges of intrusiveness and egocentricity but this seemed tolerable given that the latter offers an impression of disavowal and absurdity. All of these decisions necessitated some reflection on my part and I hope that what follows will give some insight into what is entailed by historical practice, but even that ambition is secondary to the main purpose of the book which is to provide a useful starting point for students who are interested in exploring the current state of knowledge regarding the dramatic transformations which occurred during the years of British imperial decline.

1 Anti-Colonialism in the British Empire

It is impossible to write about the end of the European empires without giving some consideration to the emergence of anti-colonial ideas in Asia, Africa and the Americas. Yet the first thing which aspiring students of anti-colonialism are likely to notice is the absence of a general text devoted to the subject. Although at one time this historiographical oversight could be ascribed to the reluctance of modern historians to engage in large projects devoted to abstract political concepts, we are now awash with semi-popular investigations of notions such as internationalism, global government, environmentalism, human rights and the Third World. Vijay Prashad's study of this last phenomenon comes closest to offering a broad overview of the non-European response to the decline of European imperialism [16]. Perhaps the negative connotations of the terminology play a part in explaining this omission, and the corollary neglect of non-alignment and the Non-Aligned Movement, whose history overlaps that of anti-colonialism, offers some corroboration for this supposition. There are difficulties in analysing a movement which is defined by what it is against, particularly when the concept against which it is defined is as large in scope and as contested as colonialism or imperialism.

Fortunately, in working on the forms which resistance to colonialism took in different territories, and in examining the lives of anti-colonial actors, historians have supplied the fragments which can be assembled to give a sense of the general significance of 20th century anti-colonialism. Recent historiographical work has emphasised the contribution made by rebels against British colonial authority to a transnational debate about what the post-colonial future should look like and how it could be obtained. Anti-colonialists took inspiration from each other and from beyond the frontiers of the British Empire. In doing so, they extended the

20th century political imagination by integrating race and culture into their critique of European supremacy and by adopting new techniques of political mobilisation. To take the three key figures examined in this chapter, Gandhi drew on both South Asian and European notions of spirituality in pioneering the tactics of non-violent resistance to authority; under the influence of his experiences in the United States, Kwame Nkrumah championed a form of pan-Africanism which resonated in Asia and the Americas; while Eric Williams utilised the expertise he had gathered in Britain, America and the Caribbean, to put history to work in the name of anti-colonialism in a way which influenced later global debates about the economics of dependency. To provide a framework for the analysis of these three influential figures the first portion of this chapter will offer a more general consideration of the themes which have emerged from recent literature on the origins, emergence and development of anti-colonial politics within the British Empire and, in particular, to the writings of the leaders of the anti-colonial movement, which constitute important source material for anyone wishing to write its history.

Historians and anti-colonialism

Historians are generally agreed that organised anti-colonial politics acquired much greater prominence in the inter-war years than before, but a bewildering number of paths are available to those wishing to trace the origins of anti-colonialism to an earlier period. The route chosen by Pankaj Mishra in a recent work of popular history entitled *From the Ruins of Empire* directs attention to the influence of men such as Jamal al-Din al-Afghani and Liang Qichao. During the late 19th century they offered both a diagnosis which explained why Asia had become subject to European authority and a prognosis about the catastrophic effects which their inferior status would have upon the peoples of the continent unless remedial measures were taken. On their account, curing Asia of the disease of European subjugation required a confrontation with imperial power [54].

For al-Afghani, who was born in 1838 in northwest Iran, the brutal aftermath of the Indian Mutiny demonstrated the necessity for an intellectual rebellion against Western ideas and a new politics of resistance to European and particularly British incursions. He responded to the persecution of Muslims, which he witnessed during the course of his extensive travels, by articulating a new and influential critique of colonialism. Mishra attends to an essay published in 1879 entitled 'The True Reason for Man's Happiness' in which al-Afghani attacked the humanitarian defence of imperialism and argued that improvements made by the British in transportation, such as the building of the railways, were simply means to exploit India more effectively, while the introduction of Western education for a minority was portrayed by al-Afghani as a way of facilitating effective colonial administration. Mishra suggests that 'This was a sophisticated idea for its time, when Indian nationalists had barely begun to formulate it' [54: 84]. It also set a precedent for later attacks on the notion of imperial humanitarianism such as those conducted by Williams in the Caribbean. Mishra acknowledges the inconsistencies in late 19th century anti-colonialism and suggests that, although in his early career al-Afghani assimilated Western progressive ideas such as constitutionalism and women's rights, later in his life he reasserted the importance of Islamic self-strengthening and the obligation of Muslims to unite under the banner of the Ottoman Caliphate. Al-Afghani's thinking thus demonstrated a tension between a conservative form of communalism, which looked backwards in upholding the paternalism and authoritarianism of precolonial societies, and the advocacy of individual rights against the impositions of the colonial state, which seemed to necessitate the transcending of older forms of political and social organisation. Similarly, another of Mishra's subjects, Liang Qichao, sometimes urged his Asian audience to emulate the West and at others recommended the rejection of European ideas in favour of reliance on Asian traditions. While acknowledging this theoretical indeterminacy, Mishra's analysis of the life and work of al-Afghani and Liang Qichao establishes the fact that new forms of anti-colonial philosophy were emerging in Asia long before the outbreak of the First World War [54].

In the manner of many popular histories, Mishra generally avoids reflection on methodological issues. By contrast, Barbara Bush, in her treatment of resistance to imperialism in inter-war Africa, attends to the contrast between traditional approaches to the subject and new postcolonial perspectives, and finds problems with both. In her view, by employing concepts such as gender, race and culture, postcolonialism remedied the narrow concern with elites evident in traditional historiography. She interprets cultural artefacts, such as the book and film of *Sanders of the River*, as part of a cultural superstructure which helped maintain British hegemony in Africa. Although by drawing attention to the power of these representations, postcolonialism helped transcend official perspectives, Bush suggests that it became too preoccupied with abstractions and, as a consequence, 'obscured or mystified real structures of economic exploitation, globalised western power and racial oppression' [19: xiii]. She therefore devotes particular attention to the coercive measures employed by the imperial state and the emergence of resistance to it in West and South Africa. Bush also criticises the earlier historiography for focusing too narrowly on post-1945 African nationalism; such an approach fails to acknowledge that 'the colonial authorities were faced with a mounting tide of popular discontent and protest during the inter-war years, which they tried to suppress through mechanisms of cultural imperialism, but also increasingly repressive policies' [19: 127]. Bush concludes that these authoritarian politics proved counter-productive and were a key factor in stimulating anti-colonial resistance.

Some of Bush's conclusions put her at odds with a more recent account of the same subject matter by Jonathan Derrick. Rather than focusing on the more coercive character of interwar colonialism, his work on those he describes in the title of his monograph as *Africa's 'Agitators'* focuses on the importation of anti-colonial ideologies from outside Africa. On his account, the two most important of these were Marxism-Leninism and black nationalism. Large portions of the book are devoted to what Derrick describes as the 'air of unreality' which pervaded the African strategy of international communists, such as the Trinidadian George Padmore. Presented with the alternatives of a struggle on behalf of the global victims of imperial exploitation and economic oppression, as advocated by Marxists such as Padmore, or a confrontation with white colonialism and racial domination, on the basis of a new philosophy of black empowerment, Africans chose the latter. In doing so they adopted and then adapted the ideas of the Jamaican political activist Marcus Garvey. Like al-Afghani's travels around Asia, Garvey's journeys around the Americas persuaded him that imperialism sapped the morale of the colonised and led them to collude in the politics of white superiority and black inferiority. Derrick suggests that 'if Garvey was strongly contested in America, far away in Africa he became a legend' [44: 88]. There is a certain tension in Derrick's own argument because the space devoted to describing links between international communism and African nationalism seems at odds with his determination to demonstrate the marginality of Lenin's legacy in comparison with that of Garvey. At various points he is forced to qualify the general argument by, for example, acknowledging communist influence in the politics of South Africa. Perhaps the most notable counter-example to Derrick's attempt to marginalise the significance of class conflict is the West African Youth League in Sierra Leone which moved beyond narrow middle-class activism to mobilise workers in Freetown [44].

Despite their differences, Mishra, Bush and Derrick all rely to some degree on the autobiographical and semi-autobiographical writings of the anti-colonial activists they study. Questions concerning the reliability and utility of this kind of writing have been a particular concern for historians and the work of Carol Polsgrove, Judith Brown and Tony Stockwell offers a representative sample of different approaches. Polsgrove endorses the postcolonial thesis that the key element in the Western subjugation of the non-Western world was the presumption by Western writers that they could speak more authoritatively about the non-Western world than the people who lived there. It was by this means that imperial subjects were effectively silenced. On Polsgrove's account, the participation by colonial subjects in the writing of their own history was a decisive moment because it changed their status: African writers of anti-colonial texts 'who had once been objects, spoken about, looked down upon, pitied or maligned had become subjects' [28: xii]. In this sense, the very act of writing and then of being published transformed these actors into 'agents in their own history'. Among the books which Polsgrove identifies as significant in re-establishing the authority of colonial subjects to speak for themselves are George Padmore's *Pan-Africanism or Communism*; Jomo Kenyatta's *Facing Mount Kenya*; the novels and memoirs of Peter Abrahams, including particularly *A Wreath for Udomo*; C. L. R. James's *Nkrumah and the Ghana Revolution*; and Nkrumah's own autobiographical account of the struggle for independence, entitled simply *Ghana*, to which we will return [44]. In *Windows into the Past*, one of Gandhi's biographers, Judith Brown, seeks to extend this argument for the significance of autobiographical and semi-autobiographical writing to a wider constituency in the context of South Asian history [1].

Although most historians writing today acknowledge the importance of incorporating the view from the periphery, autobiographical accounts written by anti-colonial activists are vulnerable to accusations of partiality and inaccuracy. This is most evident from the singular case of Chin Peng's intervention in the historiographical debate about the Malayan insurgency. His role in directing the insurrectionary forces of the Malayan Communist Party during the period 1948–1960 made him one of the most wanted men in the British Empire at a time when he was still in his mid-twenties. In the aftermath of the war he disappeared from view but in 1989 he re-emerged and set about reversing the usual procedure by which historians criticise and analyse the writings of historical actors. Chin Peng's autobiography, which was published in 2003 as *Alias Chin Peng: My Side of History*, provided a forum for him to comment unfavourably on much of the extant historiography on the basis of his own experiences and research. For example, he asserted that, contrary to the consensus in the secondary literature, the decision to launch the insurgency was a defensive one which was taken reluctantly: 'We feared walking into a British trap. The CPM [Communist Party of Malaya] leadership was convinced, and I think rightly so, that any move on our part to confront gangsterism with gangsterism would only provide Government with the tailor made excuse necessary to suppress and ultimately ban the Party.'[1] Historians were intrigued by this unprecedented intervention and many of the leading scholars of the insurgency, including Stockwell, were able to talk to him during a workshop in Canberra in 1999. Stockwell judged Chin Peng's performance during the discussions to be 'impassive, measured and generally consistent' [65: 283].

In examining the autobiography, Stockwell is cautiously sceptical about Chin Peng's revisionist enterprise and suggests that the arguments he deploys are already familiar and largely discredited. In particular, Chin Peng's portrayal of a British colonial elite determined to retain control over their Malayan patrimony at whatever cost strikes Stockwell as wholly inconsistent with the documentary record which demonstrates that the British 'were looking for a way to escape from the burdens of empire by transferring power to a reliable Malayan regime as soon as was feasible'. Stockwell suggests: '...one is tempted to conclude that in the struggle for Malaya, Chin

Peng has come second with the pen as he formerly did with the sword' [65: 297]. Stockwell's judgement of Chin Peng's testimony poses meaningful questions for postcolonial theorists who would tend to privilege such accounts on the grounds that they challenge the complacency of much traditional imperial history; but any return to orthodox methods and to an exclusive engagement with the vast archive of the imperial power raises the troubling possibility that the less easily recorded voice from the periphery will remain silent. In those circumstances the view from the metropolis will prevail by default. Many historians have taken to a critical examination of the ideas and actions of those who led rebellions against colonialism in Asia, Africa and the Americas as a means of navigating between these scholarly perils.

Mohandas Gandhi

In his book *The Un-Gandhian Gandhi,* Claude Markovits described the 'extremely rich posthumous trajectory' of the most famous 20th century critic of colonialism. After his death, the possibility of misreading Gandhi greatly added to his influence because, on a generous reading, it allowed him to be adapted to different contexts and, on a more cynical one, it allowed for the appropriation of his moral capital by the leaders of other causes. Markovits notes that there are several genuine difficulties in studying him as a historical figure rather than a legend. He lived a long life, from 1869 to 1948, and between the young Gandhi and the old Gandhi there are great differences. His intellectual biography is marked by at least two epiphanies: in the first, which occurred at some point between 1906 and 1920 depending on one's reading of his career, he lost confidence in the possibility of reforming British imperialism and, in the second, at the very end of his life, his faith in his own vision of the reform of Indian society was shattered by the violence which accompanied partition. The answer to the question of what Gandhi thought therefore depends on which part of Gandhi's life one is considering. Furthermore, although he denigrated his own abilities as a writer and celebrated the virtues of withdrawal and silence, his collected works still run to ninety-eight volumes. The process of editing this material began in 1956 and was not completed until 1994. The status of a later, revised edition of his complete works caused controversy due to the excision of some significant material. The original is an invaluable but exhausting resource which is accessible online via the *GandhiServe Foundation*.[2]

If the primary source base is extensive then the secondary commentary on Gandhi gives the illusion of unlimited scope. Book-length additions to this literature published in the West since 2010 include an orthodox biography by Jad Adams, an unorthodox and contentious analysis of Gandhi's tactics of non-violence by Faisal Devji, a mildly revisionist account of his early life in Britain and South Africa by Ramachandra Guha and a defence of his achievements which recognises his many eccentricities by Joseph Lelyveld [33; 45; 46; 49]. Vigilant Gandhi scholars have difficulty maintaining any sort of mastery over this continuous literary flow and the task is impossible for those whose primary field of expertise lies elsewhere. Such problems are compounded by the fact that any serious effort to engage with Gandhi must also acknowledge the radically different cultural context in which he operated. This is most obvious when decoding his political vocabulary. Even a preliminary reading of Gandhi's writings will yield a confounding sense that the terms he used, such as *satyagraha*, *ahimsa* and *swaraj*, lose much nuance and force when translated as truth-force, non-violence and independence. This reflects the fact that Gandhi was writing about politics from the religious traditions of Hinduism which are unfamiliar to many in the West. Although one might think that this would lend an advantage to those who share this tradition, there are perils associated with 'insider' perspectives, given that Gandhi's interpretation of Hindu texts was regarded by his contemporaries as extremely unorthodox. Furthermore, the peculiarities of his personality were the subject of as much comment from his Indian peers as from the global audience, which was later drawn to the history of his struggle with colonialism precisely because of the exceptional nature of his political performance.

This litany of caveats ought to be regarded as prudential rather than prohibitive and over the last twenty years historians have made some significant advances in analysing Gandhi's political ideas and his legacy. Historians now largely agree that his adoption of non-violence as an instrument in the anti-colonial struggle was continually contested. Devji begins his novel defence of Gandhian political theory by recalling the attacks made on his ideas by Kanji Dwarkadas, who became disillusioned by the death and destruction which accompanied the nationalist protests which Gandhi led [45]. Dennis Dalton's discussion of non-violence, which was originally published in 1993 and has recently resurfaced in a new edition, addresses the criticisms of Rabindranath Tagore and M. N. Roy. While Gandhi achieved some tactical successes by encouraging his supporters to withdraw their cooperation with the imperial authorities, his contemporaries queried his expectation that the suffering entailed by the campaign of dissidence would engender moral reform in India and a recognition of the injustice of authoritarian government in Britain. Dalton focuses on the salt march as 'one of the most dramatic events of modern Indian history' and argues that it demonstrated the creative political tactics of Gandhi as well as their efficacy [42: 91]. To the consternation of the orthodox politicians of the Congress Party Gandhi chose the Salt Act of 1882, which imposed a monopoly on production and a tax on consumption of salt, as a symbol of imperial oppression. On 12 March 1930, members of his ashram began a 200-mile procession to the coast where, 24 days later, Gandhi broke the government's stranglehold on production by collecting sea salt. His intention was to demonstrate that government revenues were dependent on denying ordinary people ready access to one of the necessities of life. News of the march sparked a mass campaign of disobedience and by the end of the year the government had imprisoned 60,000 protestors.

Dalton contends that the perplexity and ambivalence which the salt *satyagraha* elicited from the imperial authorities demonstrates the effectiveness of non-violent power in action. The resolution of the viceroy, Irwin, faltered as he contemplated the possibility that arresting Gandhi would provoke a hunger strike. Punitive measures risked further arousing the population and alienating 'moderate' Indians on whom the British relied to administer the country. More tellingly, Dalton presents evidence of the disorienting moral effect which the salt protests elicited. He cites the memoirs of a police officer, John Court Curry, who recorded: 'I had strongly disliked the necessity of dispersing these non-violent crowds and although the injuries inflicted on the law-breakers were almost invariably slight the idea of using force against such men was very different from the more cogent need for using it against violent rioters who were endangering other men's lives' [42: 133]. Curry recalls that the task made him feel nauseous. In confounding British imperial administrators in this way and influencing millions of Indians,

Dalton suggests that Gandhi answered his critics and offered a decisive example of the practicality of non-violent protest in resisting injustice.

From a Gandhian perspective the achievement of independence from Britain was inseparable from the reform of Indian society. It was for this reason that the violence which accompanied partition caused him such distress: India had achieved independence but without spiritual renewal. The conservative aspects of this vision have long been troublesome for those who wish to claim Gandhi as a progressive and are given a fresh reading by Tanika Sarkar in her analysis of his ambitions for social reform. Having established her reputation by writing about activist women, Sarkar finds that Gandhi's gender politics were a peculiar mixture of progressive and reactionary elements. The latter were a consequence both of his 'idealization of a split and gendered world', in which the public sphere was understood as male and the domestic sphere as female, and of his determined insistence that sexual abstinence was a sign of moral purity, which was a prescription which he applied with greater force to women than to men. In this sense Gandhian philosophy can be regarded as a recasting of traditional, patriarchal prejudices; but this does not allow for the new opportunities which the politics of non-violence offered to women who became influential participants in the campaign for Indian independence. Furthermore, Gandhi's insistence that his male followers should become adept at work traditionally associated with women, most notably at the spinning wheel, tended to dissolve the gender distinctions which he reaffirmed at other points. Sarkar finds a similar ambiguity in Gandhi's attitude to class antagonisms: here the conservatism of his ideas about trusteeship, in which poor peasants should look to the paternal instincts of landlords for relief from suffering, is striking. As in the case of women, however, once Gandhi translated his theories into practice the effect could be liberating. Sarkar asserts that 'Gandhi was the first Indian leader who solicited peasant entry into the political nation, enlarging its remit to constitute some of the largest mass movements in the history of the world' [63: 175].

These incongruities in Gandhi's thinking and political practice have generated many opportunities for scholars to reassess his philosophy. For example, Mithi Mukherjee has recently suggested that those commentators who are perplexed by Gandhi's ideas often fail to register that Western and Indian conceptions of freedom are and were antithetical to one another: the former interprets freedom in terms of the assertion of individual and national identity, while the latter understands the concept in terms of the renunciation or abandonment of individual identities. As a representative of the Indian tradition, 'it is not surprising that Gandhi's involvement in the twentieth-century anticolonial resistance movement was marked by a commitment to renunciative freedom as the highest goal, and at the same time by a critique of the western discourse of freedom as being partly an exercise of power, most evident in colonialism' [56: 461]. In this understanding, the key moment in Gandhi's career is the Jalianwalla Bagh massacre of 1919 and the failure of the imperial authorities to bring the perpetrators to justice. Only at this point did Gandhi finally acknowledge the futility of an appeal to Western standards of morality; as an alternative he returned to specifically Indian traditions to explore what was entailed by the politics of renunciation. Under this new theoretical dispensation, practices such as celibacy and fasting, which could be regarded as either irrelevant or auxiliary to the pursuit of liberation in a Western context, became central to Gandhi's campaign for *swaraj* or freedom. The challenge to imperialism was profound: 'Britain as the self-proclaimed agent of western civilisation faced much more in India than just another anticolonial resistance movement against the empire: it faced a challenge to its core notions of political freedom' [56: 472]. Misunderstandings have arisen because Gandhi's interpreters have continued to privilege Western understandings of freedom. Mukherjee's emphasis on this kind of occidental misreading places her in the postcolonial school and she acknowledges a debt to Chakrabarty's suggestion that European subjectivity should be provincialized [3; 56].

Mukherjee and most other commentators acknowledge that the post-independence history of India has departed widely from the goals which Gandhi set for the country. This forms one element of a lively debate about his legacy, key elements of which can be garnered from a short book by Markovits, which was translated into English as *The Un-Gandhian Gandhi* three years after its publication in France in 2000, and a longer monograph by Thomas Weber entitled *Gandhi as Disciple and Mentor*, published in 2004. Their interpretations differ in some important ways but both uncover evidence of misrepresentation in the Western historiography on

Gandhi as well as in the wider culture. They also offer concise
accounts of the roles of Vinoba Bhave and Jayaprakash Narayan
in maintaining the reforming and dissenting tradition established
by Gandhi. With regard to the global dissemination of Gandhian
ideas, Markovits detects an eagerness to rip Gandhi from his particular time and place and put him to new purposes in dramatically
different contexts. According to Markovits the ubiquitous global
presence of Gandhi is less a product of direct inspiration and more
a consequence of the ability of others to misinterpret and appropriate his ideas. This tendency is at least partially derived from the
proclivity of European and American interpreters to make Gandhi
into an icon of Christian saintliness. The trend originated in early
Western biographies and culminated in Ben Kingsley's portrayal
in Richard Attenborough's film *Gandhi*, which was more attentive
to implicit parallels with the life of Christ than to Gandhi's Hindu
reformism. On Markovits's account, the association of Gandhi
with pacifism, which is perhaps the most ingrained element of
Western portrayals, is unwarranted. Although in his later career
Gandhi did espouse the Hindu notion of *ahimsa*, this was a secondary feature associated with the search for individual spiritual
reform, or the quest for truth. Largely for tactical reasons, Gandhi
encouraged Indians to volunteer for military service in the First
World War and throughout his career 'always took care to keep a
distance vis-à-vis the pacifists though he showed some sympathy for
some of their ideas' [50: 159]. Markovits suggests we should look
for the legacy of Gandhi in more unexpected places. It is evident
for example that some of the values he espoused, such as indus-
triousness, punctuality and chastity, were those of a late Victorian
gentleman and, in that sense, he can be seen as a transmitter of
a Western notion of civic virtue into Indian society. Like Sarkar,
Markovits also credits Gandhi with some innovations in extending the scope of anti-colonial campaigns beyond the urban middle
classes. He argues that the stalemate between the nationalist movement and the imperial authorities 'could only be broken if there
arose a leader capable of capturing the energies of the peasantry
without directly subordinating them to the objectives of the bourgeoisie. This was Gandhi's achievement' [50: 145; 60].

Whereas for Markovits, Gandhi scholarship is imperilled by the
tendency to interpret him in the context of Christian ideas, for
Weber the misstep taken by many of his Western biographers is to

focus on his political career at the expense of his intimate life and spiritual development. Weber suggests that the historiographical marginalisation of Gandhi's friends and co-workers, particularly Indian friends and co-workers such as his second cousin, Maganlal Gandhi and his leading ally from the field of Indian business, Jamnalal Bajaj, has led scholars to underestimate the extent to which his ideas and campaigns were the products of mutual influence within a shared Indian culture. In thinking about Gandhi as a disciple, Western historians have tended to focus on figures who were distant in time or space, such as Leo Tolstoy and John Ruskin; as a mentor he is usually portrayed as handing on lessons to those operating in different continents, such as Martin Luther King and Kenneth Kaunda. Weber does not censure those authors who focus on this kind of transnational, intellectual genealogy, but, in contrast to Markovits, he detects in their political and philosophical preoccupations a danger of actually underestimating Gandhi's wider influence. Sub-disciplines within the academic study of ecology, peace, economics and politics have witnessed the transmission of Gandhian ideas through the agency of writers such as Arne Naess, Johan Galtung, E. F. Schumacher and Gene Sharp. In some instances, such as Sharp's technical analysis of the tactics of passive resistance and Schumacher's development of people-centred economics, Gandhi's imprint was clearly discernible at the outset, but his ideas were refined to the point where almost all traces of his initial contribution were erased. By contrast, Weber asserts that Gandhi's contribution to the development of Naess's concept of 'deep ecology' has been insufficiently acknowledged. In another case of Gandhi's importance in new academic fields, Weber goes so far as to state, 'as modern peace research is not understandable without Galtung's contribution, so Galtung's work in the area is not understandable without a knowledge of Gandhi's contribution to his thought' [67: 190].

Eric Williams

When describing the legacy of Eric Williams, the celebrated Barbadian author George Lamming pointed to the defining role which popular education played in Williams's politics: 'He turned history, the history of the Caribbean, into gossip so that the story of a people's predicament seemed no longer the infinite barren track of documents, dates and texts' [48: 731]. Certainly no other anti-colonial politician was better qualified to question the truthfulness of the uplifting imperial stories which the British liked to tell to themselves and to the colonised. In 1944, ten years before entering the political fray on his home island of Trinidad, Williams published a book entitled *Capitalism and Slavery*, which was based on a revised version of the doctoral thesis he had written at Oxford. As well as a feat of scholarship, the book was an attack on imperial complacency and there are few works of history written in the 20th century which have attracted more commentary. Much of the later analysis of the book's arguments was unsympathetic, but in 1987, Barbara Lewis Solow and Stanley L. Engerman brought together twelve historians to discuss its significance. In his concluding essay Richard Sheridan returned to the question of Williams's motives in writing history: 'He wanted to confront the educated and the wider English-speaking world with the sins of omission and commission of their forefathers and use this weapon to achieve racial, political, and social justice' [64: 325]. Slavery was an ideal topic on which to challenge the moral authority of empire and when we turn to the specifics of Williams's argument, the implications for the development of anti-colonial philosophy become apparent. Most readings of *Capitalism and Slavery* focus on its tripartite argument: that racism was an outcome of slavery rather than its cause, which was the profit motive; that the capital accumulated by means of the slave trade provided the financial foundation for the Industrial Revolution in Britain; and that the abolition of slavery in the 19th century was not the consequence of a humanitarian backlash in the metropolis but of its decreasing profitability. In a 1992 essay on the subject of the historian as politician, Paul Sutton registered the influence these arguments had on later scholars, including the Guyanese historian and political activist Walter Rodney, and notes that the argument of the book 'has moved beyond the history classroom to become the inspiration and indispensable foundation of contemporary West Indian political economy' [66: 99]. In a special issue of *Callaloo* devoted to Williams, Gerald R. Bosch goes further than Sutton and investigates how the Williams thesis could and was utilised to frame global debates about the continuing economic dependency of the former colonies on the old imperial powers. By offering an analysis which suggested that the wealth of the West was founded on the enslavement of Africans, and diminishing the significance of humanitarianism in the abolition of the slave trade, Williams provided the moral basis for later criticisms of Western economic orthodoxy by dependency theorists [38].

In his role as a Trinidadian politician, Williams deployed his prototypical version of dependency theory in his confrontations with the last generation of British colonial administrators and a new generation of American envoys. Although it was common for nationalist critics of imperialism to refer to the past sins of British rule, none was quite so determined, or so well-equipped to make the historical record serve the purposes of the present and none had quite such an intimidatory effect. For example, during the negotiations which led to Trinidad's independence, Williams argued that Britain was morally obliged to offer economic assistance to the Caribbean after independence because the wealth of the West had been accumulated from the forced labour of slaves, while the dismal economic conditions which continued in the region after emancipation were incontestably an outcome of British administrative failures. At an Inter-Governmental Conference in 1961 he told the British Colonial Secretary, Iain Macleod: 'the present discussion should begin with a clear acknowledgement by the United Kingdom Government that the present economic conditions of all the territories was their responsibility'.[3] As I suggested in *Ordering Independence* the demand for $442 million in British financial assistance for the Caribbean 'did not amount to an appeal to altruism in response to local infirmity but rested on a moral obligation to help rectify the economic problems which the British empire was handing on to the independent states' [25: 146].

While Williams was sharpening his historiographical weapons to hurl at British officials, he was also carving out a singular position on Cold War issues which would make American neo-imperialism a target for popular protest in Trinidad. Williams's campaign to eject the American navy and military from their Trinidadian enclave at Chaguaramas began in July 1957 and culminated with the famous 'march in the rain' by an army of Trinidadian citizens on 22 April 1960. At the end of the procession Williams declared the wartime agreement under which the British had granted the Americans access to Chaguaramas to be one of the seven deadly sins of colonialism and consigned a copy to the flames. Colin A. Palmer suggests that 'This anticolonial rhetoric had no precedent in the British West Indian islands' [57: 77]. Williams's actions were, on Palmer's account, influenced by the anti-colonial traditions of the United States, as encapsulated in the criticisms which President John Quincy Adams had made of European incursions into the Western hemisphere in the early 19th century. As Jason C. Parker has pointed out, Williams's populist campaigns engendered a degree of ambivalence among contemporary American policymakers: they had a long history of demanding Caribbean reform, yet reacted aggressively once Williams accused Washington of engaging in neo-colonialism [27]. In my work, I was particularly struck by the way in which Washington came to treat Williams as a pioneer of anti-Americanism in the Western hemisphere and the extent of their efforts to destabilise his government. This was a paradoxical outcome, given that Williams was a committed and long-standing opponent of Soviet penetration of the Caribbean and his party, the People's National Movement (PNM), rejected socialism. Despite his rhetorical radicalism, Williams was in many ways a more pragmatic figure than Nkrumah or Gandhi and in November 1960, to the fury of his erstwhile teacher and ally, C. L. R. James, he accepted a deal which offered Trinidad significant economic assistance as recompense for the ongoing American occupation of a smaller portion of the Chaguaramas site [52].

Whereas the expanding secondary literature on the Chaguaramas controversy focuses on the tactics Williams employed in his diplomatic confrontations with British and American power, Selwyn R. Cudjoe offers a close examination of the innovative techniques Williams devised to mobilise the people of Trinidad in support of the PNM's campaign for independence. Williams employed the open space of Port of Spain's Woodford Square as an outdoor university. Although there were no seminars or tutorials, between June 1955 and January 1956 Williams and other members of the People's Education Movement offered fifty-two lectures on a variety of historical, economic and political topics. Trinidad's culture of oral debating and the privilege it accorded to the spoken word, which was manifest in both formal debating societies and informal liming on street corners, provided a receptive environment for this kind of initiative [40]. The University of Woodford Square was not just about offering further education to the many Trinidadians who had been denied secondary or tertiary education; it was also a political instrument designed to garner support for the PNM which, under Williams's direction, won every election between 1956 and his death in 1981.

The formal speech or lecture was the means by which Williams mobilised public opinion on issues that mattered to him and Cudjoe's collection of transcripts has the entirely appropriate title *Eric E. Williams Speaks* [41]. The contrast to Gandhi, who disliked public speaking, is striking, but it was considerably easier to gather a significant proportion of the population of the small island of Trinidad to hear a speaker than was feasible in the case of the vast Indian subcontinent. Williams had travelled widely and Cudjoe argues that the anti-elitist pedagogical ideas which he implemented in Trinidad were a consequence of exposure to the practices of African-Americans who regarded education as a key component in their struggle for liberation [40]. A special issue of the *Journal of African-American History* examined Williams's experiences in the United States both as an academic who had published extensively in the same periodical when it still had the title *Journal of Negro History* and as an imperial bureaucrat working for the wartime Anglo-American Caribbean Commission. One of his recurring ideas was that the histories of Trinidad and the Caribbean were inextricably tied to wider historical processes and his work for the Commission extended his range of contacts inside and outside of the Anglophone empire. In his contribution to the volume, Tony Martin exhibits a quote from Williams stating that his visits to the Francophone and Hispanophone Caribbean at this time 'laid the foundations for my emergence as intellectual spokesman of the Caribbean peoples. I was in 1940 a West Indian who had more direct and closer contact, historically and actually, with the Caribbean area as a whole than any other' [51: 277]. This is typically self-aggrandising but Williams was proud of his proficiency in Spanish and more could certainly be written about the influence exerted on the Anglophone territories of the Caribbean by liberationist thinkers such as the Cuban José Marti and reformers such as Munoz Marin in Puerto Rico.

Although Williams's biographers exhibit some interest in his intellectual influences, they have often been more concerned with critical discussion of his personality and how this manifested itself in his successes and failures in the public arena. Selwyn Ryan's monumental biography of 2008, which runs to over 800 pages, attempts to come to a balanced judgement but implicates Williams in some significant setbacks in Caribbean politics. This is most evident in Ryan's criticisms of the contribution Williams made to ongoing regional disunity by refusing to assume the leadership of the federation of the West Indies after Jamaica seceded in 1961. Ryan emphasises the dismay of Caribbean elites when Trinidad opted to follow Jamaica out of the federation, which had been formed only three years earlier: 'They were shocked to find that their intellectual leader had proven to be every whit as insular as those he had once chastised' [61: 238]. He cites the judgement of one of the most famous intellectuals of the era, Arthur Lewis, that the 'awful' leadership of West Indian politicians was responsible for collapse of the federation and the subsequent history of political fragmentation [61: 253].

Like many other Caribbean politicians Williams's style is often described as charismatic and Ken Boodhoo characterised the self-obsession which often accompanies such an approach: 'the force which drove him seemed to be a yearning for the redress of griev-ances which represented a narcissistic injury to his self-image' [37: 132]. Anybody who reads those passages of his memoir *Inward Hunger* devoted to the racist slights he experienced during his stud-ies at Oxford will find some corroboration for this view.[4] Patricia Mohammed has also analysed Williams as a charismatic leader and suggests his success as an anti-colonial politician was partly deter-mined by the gender stereotypes prevalent in colonial Trinidad. She finds that a 'thick thread that runs through the writings and speeches of William is the metaphoric discourse on masculinity' [55: 178]. This was particularly evident in his thinking about black African-Trinidadian men and the white colonial 'massa', whose rela-tionship 'is that between a subordinated masculinity and a hegem-onic one'. The role of women also came to the fore in Williams's psephological calculations. His series of electoral victories can, in part, be attributed to his appeal to a female middle- and working-class constituency. In some respects, most notably the promotion of sexual equality within the PNM, Williams demonstrated an affinity with feminism, but Mohammed argues that much of what he did reflected 'the fundamental belief in the superiority of male leadership' [55: 187]. The final word ought, however, to go to Ryan, who lived through much of the Williams era. Although critical of him in many respects, he expresses admiration for the manner in which Williams's anti-colonial activism 'gathered all the inchoate forces into one movement that could not be resisted'. Ryan concludes that 'his performance was worthy of History's applause' [61: 782–786].

Kwame Nkrumah

While Eric Williams made his reputation as a historian before he entered politics, Kwame Nkrumah attempted to validate his credentials as a social scientist after he became the first Prime Minister of an independent Ghana. He was particularly eager to establish a firm philosophical foundation for his concept of Positive Action, which was the label he gave to the campaign of civil disobedience that he had initiated in the colonial Gold Coast in 1950. In *Consciencism*, which was published in 1964, he even offered an algebraic representation of the relationship between Positive Action and the colonial state:

$$col.g. \longleftrightarrow (na > pa)\, g$$

Consulting the glossary of symbols which Nkrumah provides in the text reveals that *g* stands for a territory, *col.g.* stands for a territorial colony and *na* and *pa* stand for negative and positive action. Ever more elaborate equations follow.[5] Although historians may view such an exercise with scorn, the employment of this kind of formula reflects the academic sway exerted by the algebraic equations of game theorists such as Thomas Schelling and Herman Kahn in the 1960s. Furthermore, the thought expressed in the initial equation, which is that a country's colonial status derives from the prevalence of negative over positive action raises some practical questions about the methods nationalists used to obtain independence. Even if the manner of their expression might now appear antiquated, Nkrumah's political ideas have attracted the attention of scholars interested in the tactics and strategy of anti-colonial struggle.

Kwame Botwe-Asamoah is an unabashed partisan of the ideas underpinning *Consciencism* in which, he suggests, Nkrumah 'emphasizes the highest ideals underlying the traditional African society, and argues for the restoration of the spirit of classical African cultural values to bear on the new Africa' [39: 85].

Botwe-Asamoah indicates that such ideas were underappreciated both by his own teachers in Ghana, who associated Nkrumah with communism, and by Western scholars such as Robert July, whose work on Africa he finds particularly objectionable. In his conclusion, he places Nkrumah alongside Frantz Fanon, Sékou Touré and Amilcar Cabral as one of a group of thinkers who reasserted the importance of African culture in resisting colonialism. Nkrumah's particular contribution was to provide an account of the relationship between the humanist character of the African personality and the pursuance of socialist politics. Botwe-Asamoah states: 'under socialism the study and master of nature has a humanist impulse directed not toward profiteering, but the affording of ever increasing satisfaction for the material and spiritual needs of the greater number of the African people' [39: 211]. This emphasis on humanism and socialism leads to a surprising neglect of pan-Africanism in Botwe-Asamoah's account. By contrast, Ama Biney gives the continental implications of his ideas much greater prominence in her analysis of Nkrumah's legacy. Although in one article she describes Nkrumah as 'the Nelson Mandela of the 1950s and 1960s', the monograph Biney published in 2011 provides a more cautious and qualified defence of his ideas than this might betoken [35]. She contends that scholars such as Botwe-Asamoah belong to a hagiographical tradition but that even a critical examination of Nkrumah's ideology reveals the congruence between his political philosophy and his actions. In works such as *Africa Must Unite* and *Neo-Colonialism: The Last Stage of Imperialism*, which were published before *Consciencism*, during his years as President of Ghana, Nkrumah offered an early and effective articulation of theories of pan-Africanism and economic dependency. On Biney's account the enduring character of these ideas is evident from the continued appeal of greater continental unity based on African rather than European models of development. Events which took place long after his death, such as the institutional transformation of the Organisation of African Unity (OAU) into the African Union (AU) in 2002, continue to bear Nkrumah's imprint [36].

Nkrumah's most persistent critic has been Ali Mazrui. In 1966 he described how the Ghanaian leader had welded monarchism onto Bolshevik revolutionary practice to become a Leninist Czar. This seemed an unlikely thesis, and it was published in a relatively obscure journal called *Transition*, but it attracted a great deal of attention because it coincided with the ousting of Nkrumah in a military coup. Mazrui provided evidence both of the inspiration which Nkrumah drew from Russian revolutionary practice and of his ostentatious style of government which did seem to invite parallels with the traditions of European royalism. According to Mazrui, Nkrumah's acolytes in Uganda attempted to hound him out of the country after the article was published. During the course of the Aggrey-Fraser-Guggisberg Memorial Lectures which he delivered at the University of Ghana in 2004, Mazrui reasserted the validity of his original thesis. While endorsing some of his ideas about continental solidarity, Mazrui claimed that as a Leninist Czar, Nkrumah had set the precedent for one-party rule in Africa. In this interpretation, the path from Nkrumah in Ghana to Mugabe in Zimbabwe was short and direct. Each of these autocrats asserted that African traditions of communalism and consensus warranted one-party rule in a way that was not easily understood by those from a Western political tradition founded on individualism and competition between parties. These affinities were emphasised by Mazrui to justify the argument that Nkrumah 'started the whole tradition of Black authoritarianism in the postcolonial era. He was the villain of the piece' [53: 3].

Biney responds to these accusations with a two-fold strategy: she acknowledges their force, while seeking to contextualise them within an emergent tendency towards developmentalist authoritarianism in Africa. Establishing a one-party state in Ghana was, Biney acknowledges, an example of Nkrumah's autocratic tendencies, but other African leaders, whether on the right or left of the political spectrum, had independently reached similar conclusions at the same moment, including Sékou Touré of Guinea, Félix Houphouët-Boigny of Ivory Coast, Léopold Senghor of Senegal, Modibo Keïta of Mali, Julius Nyerere of Tanganyika and Jomo Kenyatta of Kenya. On this interpretation, rather than a pioneer of Leninist autocracy, Nkrumah was one of a group of nationalists responding to the same structural factors which seemed to require political unity at independence. Biney cautiously suggests that Nkrumah's unwillingness to authorise capital punishment as a means of maintaining the one-party state in Ghana indicates that his authoritarianism was less thoroughgoing than that of his contemporary and rival, Félix Houphouët-Boigny, who executed thirteen of his opponents in 1963 [36].

Continuing interest in Nkrumah's legacy reflects ongoing concerns about the prevalence of African autocracy despite a countervailing trend in some countries towards parliamentary democracy. Unsurprisingly much of this discussion has focused on the period between Ghana's independence in 1957 and Nkrumah's overthrow in 1966. Turning to the literature on Nkrumah's earlier career as an anti-colonial activist and political dissident, a tension is evident between those who emphasise the innovative tactics he employed in order to secure liberation and those who regard his attitude to his opponents during the independence struggle as the harbinger of a future dictatorship. Prominent among the first group are Basil Davidson, who published *Black Star* in 1973 and C. L. R. James, whose *Nkrumah and the Ghana Revolution* first appeared in 1977: both are exceptionally vivid accounts, which take cognisance of the criticisms levelled at Nkrumah's conduct in office but offer predominantly heroic renditions of his struggle against colonialism [43; 47]. In common with the literature on Gandhi and Williams, James and Davidson commend Nkrumah's achievement in enabling the mass of the people to participate in politics for the first time. His notion of Positive Action borrowed from Gandhi's *satyagraha* campaigns but placed greater emphasis on the requirement for institutional organisation, in the form of the Convention People's Party (CPP). Davidson describes the aftermath of the meeting at Saltponds on 12 June 1949, at which Nkrumah explained his reasons for forming the CPP, as a decisive period: 'until now, nobody had spoken of modern politics, the politics of nationalism. The nation of Ghana was not yet born. But these were its months of conception' [43: 69–70]. James takes up a quote from Nkrumah that 'the market-women made the party' in order to demonstrate that Nkrumah was organising a revolution from below in which ordinary people became the envoys of the nationalist message [47: 131]. James and Davidson have tended to overshadow much later work but the noted Ghanaian scholar and politician Yakubu Saaka has elaborated on the same themes. He stresses the formation of youth wings and women's groups within the CPP as a means of political mobilisation. On Saaka's account, Nkrumah's key political accomplishment was to get ordinary people involved in politics after generations of exclusion by the British [62].

A counter-trend is represented by the work of Richard Rathbone, who argues that Nkrumah's version of anti-colonialism exacerbated divisions within Ghanaian society. He gives particular emphasis to the way in which Nkrumah's charismatic style of leadership undermined the authority of traditional elites who had reached what they regarded as a satisfactory accommodation with colonialism [58]. In reviewing the events which accompanied the celebrations of fifty years of independence in 2007, Rathbone drew attention to the 'distinctive unhappiness which swirled around Ghana's last days as the British colonial territory of the Gold Coast' [59: 705]. This disharmony was manifest in the efforts of Nkrumah's opponents in the National Liberation Movement (NLM) to delay independence. Jean Allman has examined the extent of this resistance to Nkrumah in the central and northern regions of Ghana. Secessionist sentiment in Asante took militant form in the activities of the nkwankwa or 'youngmen' who were more assertive in promoting separatism than older, traditional leaders. This younger generation believed the British governor was complicit in Nkrumah's efforts to weaken Asante autonomy and centralise power in the coastal capital of Accra. At one point, one of their activists chose to occupy the governor's official car 'as a popular declaration of Asante's right to confiscate or reclaim that very symbol of colonial officialdom, the Governor's limousine' [34: 275]. In these accounts the British are portrayed more as arbiters of local disputes than as an overbearing authority; Donald S. Rothchild, for example, criticises the colonial authorities not for procrastination but for the ineffectiveness of their efforts to mediate between Nkrumah and the NLM [60]. One of the oddities of this kind of analysis is that it often treats the formation of rival parties to the CPP as an exceptional event, yet the emergence of fractious multiparty politics in the years before independence was common, as the examples of the Democratic Labour Party in Trinidad, the Kenya African Democratic Union in Kenya and the Muslim League in India demonstrate. More systematic comparison of party formation in the late colonial era might prove a fruitful line of enquiry for students interested in institutional innovation at the end of empire. Even in the absence of such studies it is evident that party formation in the periphery was one of the most significant modifications to existing colonial practice and that it formed one aspect of the wider phenomenon of mass mobilisation practised by Gandhi, Williams and Nkrumah.

Conclusions

An examination of anti-colonialism provides an opportunity for historians to engage with the politics of the end of the British Empire, without relying on traditional narratives about the making of policy in the imperial metropolis. By adopting a global perspective and studying the exchange of ideas across and beyond colonial frontiers, historians have uncovered a different kind of transformation from the transfer of power to newly independent governments. Measured in these transnational terms the most significant development of the last years of the British Empire was the emergence of new forms of political activism; at a tactical level, this entailed mobilising colonial subjects who had never participated in politics before, and, at a strategic level, the setting of novel and more ambitious goals, which required that independence be measured in cultural and economic, as well as political, terms. Critics from the periphery, including Dwarkadas, Ryan and Mazrui, have offered some unflattering judgements regarding the parochial impact of figures such as Gandhi, Williams and Nkrumah, and this has generated a dialectic or conversation regarding their reputations which has emphasised the innovative tactics of the leaders of the anti-colonial movement in mobilising mass support for their campaigns and the influence exerted by anti-colonial politicians in fields beyond politics and in territories beyond the imperial periphery [61; 53]. Hence Gandhi's *satyagraha* was not just an influence on the likes of King in the United States or Nkrumah and Kaunda in Africa, but shaped the evolution of peace studies and ecology in the West; Williams's critique of colonial economics formed part of a Latin American debate about development economics which has fed into ongoing arguments about the inequities of global capitalism, while Nkrumah's advocacy of pan-Africanism and justification of one-party rule remain central to present debates about unity and democracy taking place across the continent. Having established that we ought not to think of the end of empire merely in metropolitan terms, it might be regarded as incongruous to turn back to the high politics of the end of empire in Britain. But as one of the leading historians of that subject has suggested, 'British anti-colonialism was in a sense an offshoot of a massive global upsurge of sentiment, which has dominated much of the history of this century' [72: 15]. Still more tellingly domestic debates about Britain and Britishness have increasingly had to contend with questions about the pervasiveness of imperial culture and its origins outside Europe. Consequently, the next chapter will move from considering the impact of peripheral developments on the wider world to scrutinising their impact in the imperial metropolis and on ideas of Britishness.

2 Britain and Britishness

Anniversaries, either in the form of commemoration or celebration, are one of the most significant ways in which the past intrudes into the culture of the present. In the case of the British Empire these intrusions are becoming more frequent. Although it initially appeared that the centenary marking of the outbreak of the First World War would focus exclusively on the trenches and the home front, the BBC eventually recognised the imperial dimension of the conflict, which included the deployment of over a million Indian soldiers and nearly half a million Canadian troops, with the broadcast of David Olusoga's two-part documentary *Forgotten Soldiers of Empire*. Olusoga was able to extend his discussion of the role of soldiers from the European colonies in his book-length study, *The World's War* [15]. But it is also possible to look for the imperial legacy in more unexpected places. When the time came in 2013 to celebrate the 50th anniversary of the BBC's science fiction institution, *Doctor Who*, Simon Winder took the opportunity to explain how the fortunes of the early Doctors were tied to those of the declining British Empire. On Winder's account, William Hartnell, Patrick Troughton and Jon Pertwee were 'specifically imperial figures', comparable to the harassed district officers who had maintained empire into the 20th century: 'He is constantly sorting out warring tribes, educating them, introducing new technologies.'[1] Winder's intervention illustrates the way in which British culture was shaped by imperial history and this has become an ever more significant feature of the historiography on decolonisation, as exemplified by a recent essay collection which assessed the reverberating effects of imperial decline on the work of a number of British authors, from the once-popular crime stories of Josephine Tey to the currently fashionable literary novels of Alan Hollinghurst [102].

Discussion of the impact of empire on artistic expression in the metropolis is now so common that the secondary literature tends to give the impression that the empire had a larger place in British culture than in British politics. This is as much a consequence of the inattentiveness of political historians to imperial themes, as of the industry and energy that cultural historians have invested in the subject. Over the last two decades appraisals of the fortunes of the two dominant political parties have tended to cast the empire to the margins. One volume entitled *Conservative Century*, which featured 20 contributions, did not include an essay on imperial policy [91]. Centenary collections dealing with the British Labour Party's history at the start of the 21st century were somewhat less neglectful but it was notable that in one compendium of 12 essays, Stephen Howe, as the leading expert on the topic, was obliged to deal with Labour's attitude to colonialism under the rubric of international affairs [74]. Although this kind of quibbling may have the air of special pleading and such editorial decisions can be justified because imperial affairs were an inconspicuous feature of British general elections, it is worth noting that the relatively small number of historians who have examined the place of empire in the history of British political organisations and parties have offered some striking and consequential findings. This chapter will examine some of this commentary before exploring how historians have interpreted the cultural impact of colonialism on notions of Britishness in the 20th century.

British politics

The left

To what extent was the colonial policy of the British Labour Party distinct from that of the Conservative Party? How sympathetic was the metropolitan labour movement to the methods and goals of anti-colonial nationalism? These two questions, presented here in the familiar style of undergraduate essay titles, cover the principal preoccupations of those who have investigated the attitudes to imperialism of the 20th century British left. In responding to the first of them, it might be argued that the continuities between periods of Labour and Conservative government on matters of colonial policy demonstrate that moderates in those parties shared similar ideas. This is the position adopted by Richard C. Whiting who suggests that liberal values prevailed when British politicians debated matters of colonial policy. On his account, left-leaning Conservatives and right-leaning Labour politicians marginalised the pro-imperialist right and the radical critics of empire on the left. The precedent for such bipartisanship was established by the Montagu-Chelmsford report of 1918, which recommended a gradual transfer of power and responsibility to Indian politicians. According to Whiting, support for this kind of incremental constitutional reform established the basis for a largely non-partisan and technical approach to decolonisation which appealed to Labour as well as Conservative leaders. Consensus politics was sufficiently durable to survive numerous controversies and was still in place at the end of the period when the Thatcher government finally implemented a plan for black majority rule in Rhodesia, despite the longstanding sympathy of many right-wing Conservative back-benchers for the white settler minority. Whiting acknowledges some of the more contentious episodes in the history of British domestic debates about empire, including the Government of India Act of 1935, the creation of the Central African Federation in 1953 and the Suez crisis of 1956, but regards such factionalist outbreaks as the exception rather than the rule [97].

Whiting's emphasis on consensus may portend a return to an earlier orthodoxy which has been rejected by other authors. Writing in 1993, Stephen Howe criticised scholars of imperialism for constructing 'an essentially consensual model of British politics as it related to colonial issues'. Despite offering many criticisms of socialist and communist policy, Howe contends that 'anticolonialism was perhaps the only issue on which the British left appeared to secure unequivocal victories during the 1950s and 1960s' [72: 18–19]. Approaching similar conclusions to Howe by other paths, Paul Kelemen and Kenneth O. Morgan have both argued that the 1950s witnessed a decisive change in metropolitan debates about empire. Kelemen suggests that groups such as the Fabian Colonial Bureau (FCB) and the Movement for Colonial Freedom (MCF) contributed to a new way of thinking about economic development in the imperial periphery. Although the 1957 Labour Party conference rejected the MCF's proposals for the nationalisation of all companies with large colonial holdings, it endorsed the principle that even small colonial territories ought to attain independence [76]. In the specific case of Kenya the Labour left 'transmitted African nationalist demands to the political elite in London, exerting pressure for reform on the government and on its own party leadership'. Long-standing criticisms of the exploitative mode of settler economics, including the application of the colour bar and the warping of taxation and infrastructure arrangements to suit the interests of white Kenyan farmers, were lent urgency by the outbreak of the Mau Mau rebellion in 1952. On Kelemen's account, it was the MCF's critique of the economic and political impact of settler colonialism, combined with a new assertiveness in African demands for independence, which 'generated a political momentum that brought the Labour movement round to supporting African nationalist aspirations' [77].

Morgan also acknowledges the role of the FCB and the MCF in developing a persuasive critique of British colonial policy. He emphasises the role of key individuals on the party's front bench and in particular James Callaghan, who acted as Shadow Colonial Secretary during Labour's years of opposition and whose biography Morgan published in 1997 [80]. During the course of the 1950s, Morgan suggests, 'Labour evolved a coherent, powerful critique of colonial affairs, one that helped create a cross-party consensus and effect the rapid demise of an empire that had lasted for 300 years' [238]. In Parliament Callaghan repeatedly discomforted Conservative ministers over colonial issues, most notably in exposing the injustices arising from their appeasement of settler interests in the Central African Federation. A measure of congruence with Whiting's later work is evident in Morgan's emphasis on the 'pragmatism and balance' of Labour policy: public attacks on Conservative colonial policy were accompanied by private efforts to encourage African nationalists to moderate their demands [81: 249].

Even if there was a measure of continuity when one government handed over to another, the terms of the debate about colonialism in 1980 were clearly very different from what they had been in 1918 and the transformation needs to be accounted for. In *Anticolonialism in British Politics* Howe criticises an earlier generation of historians for failing to register the powerful effect that the new language of anti-colonialism had upon the conduct of imperial affairs. This is a serious oversight because, Howe argues, 'British reactions to more recent events – to the Falklands or Gulf

wars, to British race relations, or the end of South African apartheid – cannot be fully understood except in relation to the experience of decolonization and the legacy of empire' [72: ix]. In terms
of domestic British politics this legacy is one of greater conflict
than is sometimes allowed; but Howe certainly does not present a
picture of a united left offering a coherent ideological challenge
to a complacent establishment. His attitude to the ideological
claims of British socialists is sceptical and this shades into disdain
when he deals with communist opportunism on colonial issues.
Although arguments about colonial policy are acknowledged as
'ideological questions par excellence', Howe finds that the moral
force of the British brand of anti-colonialism owed more to older
ethical traditions than to newly minted reinterpretations of Marx
or Lenin. In terms of its impact, Howe suggests that metropolitan
anti-colonialism created 'accountability by proxy'. This concept is
unveiled in the final sentence of the book, and encapsulates the
notion that, at a time when nationalists in the periphery had no
forum in which to hold the imperial executive to account, it was
the responsibility of the metropolitan critics of empire to represent their grievances. Instances of this tendency are evident in,
for example, the interventions of Labour MPs during parliamentary debates about the 1938 workers' rebellion in Trinidad. James
Maxton offered the House of Commons a heroic portrayal of the
Caribbean trade unionist, Uriah Butler, who was usually portrayed
as an irresponsible agitator by British administrators. Aneurin
Bevan went further and 'charged that revelations about West India
conditions wholly destroyed the claim that Britain was a better and
more humane colonial overlord than the other European powers'
[72: 98–99].

Although squabbles among themselves and with colonial nationalists sometimes vitiated the arguments of metropolitan leftists,
Howe anticipates Morgan's suggestion that by the 1950s the British
critique of colonialism had finally gathered coherence and gained
traction in Parliament. He differs from Morgan in attributing this
change in the parliamentary climate 'to the new and more active
part played by left-wing Labour MPs', clustered together in the MCF,
rather than to the party leadership [72: 252]. This aspect of Howe's
argument is supported by quantitative analysis which reveals that
by 1957, members of the MCF asked nearly half of the Commons
questions about colonial affairs. In marked contrast to Morgan, he

identifies 'the poor performance of Labour's colonial front bench', including Callaghan, as an inhibiting factor in the development of the anti-colonial argument and suggests 'they tended to enter the field only after a back-bencher such as Brockway or Sorensen had opened a breach' [72: 256].

As Howe acknowledges, metropolitan debates about colonialism were not simply a question of the British left debating with itself, but of a dialogue between critics of empire in the metropolis and in the periphery; and this was a colloquy which frequently took the form of a quarrel. An extended treatment of these disagreements has been offered by Nicholas Owen in his work on the British left's attitude to Indian politics. The great difficulty in establishing a more harmonious relationship between apparently natural allies was the inability of the British left to conceive that the nationalists of the Indian National Congress should want to depart from the model which was offered by the history of the British Labour Party. Their judgements were provincial in the sense that they took a particular parochial experience of politics in Britain and expected to find it replicated in India. Owen comments: 'nothing stands out from Labour discussions of India more strongly than the constant effort of Labour leaders to explain Congress to their followers and themselves in familiar, British terms' [87: 10]. For example, the mobilisation of the peasantry became an integral element in Indian nationalist politics in a way which had no parallel in Britain. Even strikes, to which British trade unionists were accustomed, seemed to acquire different connotations when they took place in the colonies; to their jaundiced eye, industrial relations in India appeared less about improvements in workers' conditions and more about the pursuit of grand, and often misguided, political ambitions.

When the Indian movement failed to conform to British expectations, its leaders were branded as irresponsible and this is most evident in the scepticism with which the Gandhian movement was greeted. Of all the critics of empire, Gandhi was the most insistent that decolonisation required not merely the acquisition of independence but a severance of those ties which kept India bound to European aspirations. He was determined that Indians must seize control of their own destiny rather than rely on sympathisers elsewhere to advance their cause. Owen demonstrates that these Gandhian innovations proved thoroughly disorienting for the

British left. Although there were a handful of British sympathisers within the party, Gandhi's oppositionist stance exasperated
Labour leaders and this tendency became still more pronounced
during the MacDonald and Attlee governments. Frustrated by his
inability to secure a compromise in the 1929–1931 period, Ramsay
MacDonald concluded that Gandhi's tactics made any resolution
of the nationalist question impossible. When Gandhi launched the
Quit India movement in 1942, Labour ministers consented to the
arrest of the nationalist leadership. Clement Attlee went as far as to
assert that there was a 'degree of totalitarianism in the Congress
Party' and questioned whether they would maintain a democratic
system once independence was obtained [87: 280].

Without explicitly acknowledging the affinities, Murray Steele
has offered an account of Labour's policies toward the Central
African Federation (CAF) which embraces many of the themes
adumbrated by Owen and Howe. The federation of Nyasaland,
Northern Rhodesia and Southern Rhodesia in 1953 became a
focus of criticism by African nationalists and metropolitan anti-
colonialists. It was no secret that, as a demographic minority within
a largely autonomous state, the white settlers of Southern Rhodesia
regarded federalism as a means of extending their regional
influence, in collaboration with the smaller white minorities of
Northern Rhodesia and Nyasaland. Yet the original concept of
federation had been promoted by the Labour Colonial Secretary,
Arthur Creech Jones, as what Steele calls 'a middle way between
South African apartheid and exclusive black nationalism'. The
Attlee government had envisaged a new multi-racial ethic in which
politics was no longer arranged around a confrontation between
a white minority and a black majority but focused on the kinds
of economic and social debates which purportedly transcended
racial politics. As in the case of the Congress campaign for independence, the British Labour leadership accused African political
activists of intransigence. The uncompromising tactics of black
nationalists inside the CAF irritated Marjorie Nicholson of the
FCB, who complained 'we have not been able to make them understand that a purely negative line of policy is not the most effective
in the context of British politics' [93: 138]. Although the party's
anti-colonial left protested, Attlee committed Labour to making
the federation work and Steele argues that this hindered efforts
to develop an effective critique of the Conservative government's

colonial policy during the 1950s. African nationalists certainly regarded the reformist vision of Labour politicians as hopelessly naive at a time when systematic discrimination against the black majority in employment and education continued to thrive. In that sense Steele is at odds with Morgan's belief that the declining fortunes of the federation provided an unmissably large target for the Labour opposition [81; 93].

Despite such differences in interpretation the scholarship on the anti-colonialism of the British left has given us a provisional answer to the second of the two questions posed at the outset of this discussion: the metropolitan labour movement exhibited a paternal, rather than a fraternal, form of sympathy for independence movements in Africa, Asia and the Americas which could easily be interpreted as imperial condescension. But in spite of these limitations, critics on the left did play a significant role in altering the terms of the British debate about imperialism. Whiting suggests that the response of the Conservative Party to this new critique of colonialism was pragmatic and an assessment of this claim requires an examination of the literature about the British right.

The right

Over 20 years ago Sue Onslow pointed to the centrality of 'Britain and empire' to internal tensions within the Conservative Party, from the controversy over tariff reform which began in 1903, to the fraught arguments about Rhodesia in the 1960s and 1970s. Yet the subject of the right's attitude towards empire during the 20th century remains in need of further elucidation. Much of the relatively small extant historiography focuses on the impact of particular personalities, most notably Winston Churchill and Leo Amery, during the interwar period [71; 75; 78; 95]. Biographical work of this kind presupposes that the crucial context for policymaking is provided by the lives of the people making policy but this is rarely made explicit in such interventions. Stuart Ball is an exception and he offers the most fully developed defence of the idea that imperial history can be enriched by exposing the connections between the private and public lives of politicians. In making the case for the relevance of this kind of 'intimate history' he focuses on the personal animosity between Harold Macmillan and Lord Salisbury, who resigned from Macmillan's Cabinet in

March 1957. Ball suggests that the conflict between the two men 'dominated much of the prime minister's thinking on the empire throughout his premiership' [68: 102].

Philip Murphy, who is the biographer of Macmillan's first Colonial Secretary, Alan Lennox-Boyd, has also provided a wider appreciation of the distinctive nature of Conservative imperial policy through a study of the party's African policy and his work provides perhaps the best point of entry for those wishing to understand the wider domestic context [83]. The thrust of Murphy's argument is that any crude notion that Conservative politicians, white European settlers and business interests with major investment in the colonies formed a right-wing bloc of opinion distorts a much more nuanced picture. Each of those groups was characterised by internal divisions and they sometimes made surprising alliances. For example, the decision by the government of the Central African Federation to establish a lobbying operation in London called *Voice and Vision* attracted, as might be expected, support from right-wing MPs who were predisposed to support the settlers. Less predictably, the origins of *Voice and Vision* were in growing distrust between mining companies operating inside the CAF and the federal government which resented the overbearing influence exerted by overseas investors. Furthermore, a number of liberal Conservatives objected to the CAF government's obtrusive lobbying activities, while some Labour MPs were willing to enlist for African tours organised by *Voice and Vision* [84].

Despite this blurring of the party divide, Murphy's analysis corroborates the conclusion that Labour's promotion of anti-colonialism had by the 1950s placed the Conservative Party on the defensive. Even before he became Colonial Secretary, Iain Macleod warned Macmillan that Labour's new emphasis on colonial liberation left the Conservatives in a 'difficult position' with regard to the impending general election of 1959 [84: 174]. Murphy argues that this period marked a watershed, after which pro-imperial sentiment within the party was marginalised. However, if it was marginalised it was also entrenched. A new organisational bastion for the right, the Monday Club, was founded in September 1961 by Paul Bristol of the Chelsea Conservative Association and was sponsored by Macmillan's nemesis, Lord Salisbury. Members of the Monday Club emerged as parliamentary advocates of white settler interests in Rhodesia and opponents of non-white immigration into Britain. The ideological overlap between the 'orthodox right' of the Conservative Party and what is generally labelled the 'extreme right' has not been adequately explored and this reflects a wider reticence among political historians about examining the impact of doctrines of racial superiority on party politics. The partial exceptions to this generalisation are Mark Pitchford and Mark Stuart. The former does not cover imperial themes in great detail but, in his survey of right-wing politics in the 30 years after 1945, he examines the efforts of Conservative Central Office to stymie the emerging alliance between the Monday Club and the National Front. In the 1950s, party organisers were cognisant of the dangers posed by the tiny and fascistic League of Empire Loyalists whose opposition to decolonisation appealed to some of the party's right wing supporters. The flourishing of explicit racism after Enoch Powell's Rivers of Blood speech posed an even more dangerous threat to the party's positioning in the political mainstream on questions of colonialism and immigration. Pitchford notes that from this moment 'a growing realisation of an increased connection between the extreme right outside and within the party became of serious concern' [89: 225].

Stuart focuses on Conservative opposition to the Wilson government's imposition of economic sanctions against the Rhodesian government of Ian Smith. Anticipating constitutional changes which would empower the country's black majority, in November 1965 Smith made a Unilateral Declaration of Independence (UDI) in an effort to guarantee white settler interests. Stuart concludes that the prolonged and factionalised quarrel over Rhodesia 'illustrated just how long it took the Conservative Party to get over the loss of Empire and to deal calmly with the issue of race' [94: 81]. Rhodesia was a matter on which the extreme and orthodox right found common cause. As Pitchford notes, the first leader of the National Front, A.K. Chesterton, had attempted to organise sanctions-busting shipments to Rhodesia and support for Smith alongside opposition to the Race Relations Act, constituted one of the organisation's early causes [89]. On the orthodox right, Duncan Sandys, the former Conservative Colonial Secretary, sought to turn opposition to sanctions into a popular cause through his *Peace with Rhodesia* movement. Sandys believed the party would enhance its electoral prospects by appealing to a British constituency who regarded the settlers as a besieged minority. In January 1967 he organised a rally in Trafalgar Square which was unprecedented in the history of right-wing politics but which has been largely overlooked in the historiography. The draft of the speech made by the Conservative MP and leading Smith sympathiser, John Biggs-Davison, noted: 'Today we make political history. For the first time a group of Conservative Members of Parliament have held a meeting in Trafalgar Square. This is an exceptional event.'[2] The attempt to reclaim the square, which was traditionally a forum for protests against the Suez and Vietnam wars, was at best partially successful, but the rally did demonstrate the continuing domestic saliency of colonial politics. Supporters of the Monday Club spent £90 on banners and waved these plush items at the counter-demonstrators from the Young Liberals and Young Socialists. The speakers were drowned out by chants of 'Wilson Out' on one side and 'Smith Out' on the other. Fighting spread down Whitehall and 11 arrests were made. Following the intervention of mounted police *The Times* reported: 'Downing Street was left in a litter of torn slogans, discarded shoes, broken wood and horse dung.'[3]

The precedent for this kind of rightist populism had been established by groups such as the India Defence League which organised extra-parliamentary campaigns against Indian constitutional reform in the early 1930s. Currently the most perceptive analysis of these controversies is offered by Andrew Muldoon who integrated elements of cultural theory into his account of the six years of political conflict which attended the passage of the 1935 Government of India Act. Although he does not explicitly discuss postcolonialism, his animating principle, that British views were predicated on a series of stereotypes about Indian society that distinguished it from metropolitan civilisation, suggests the influence of Edward Said. I have suggested elsewhere that it is relatively rare to find these techniques applied to an analysis of the high politics of imperialism but Muldoon is a significant exception [14]. Although his focus narrows as he proceeds, in the early sections of *Empire, Politics and the Creation of the 1935 India Act*, he demonstrates the prevalence of various forms of British cultural prejudice concerning the authenticity of Indian village life and the inauthenticity of nationalism. New organisations which sprang up on the right of British politics contended that imperialism in India was a safeguard against the dominance of indigenous Hindu elites. Some went so far as to predict that Congress rule in India would be comparable to that of the Nazis in Germany on the basis that it would place 'the dumb and helpless millions of India under the heel of their hereditary oppressors' [82: 188]. Contrary to many earlier interpretations, Muldoon argues that the grant of dominion status to the territories of white settlement, such as Australia and Canada, generated misgivings within the Conservative Party about the demission of power. De Valera's successes in Ireland, which culminated in his abolition of the Oath of Allegiance, seemed to confirm that dominionhood offered inadequate protection for British influence. On Muldoon's account, Conservative rebelliousness on India was underpinned by the fear that constitutional reform would culminate in the emergence of an Indian dominion and an 'Indian de Valera.' The National Government operated under constant fear of parliamentary defeat and he concludes that the bill was only passed because the less diehard rebels feared splitting the party [82].

Muldoon's analysis is congruent with that of Owen, who suggests that the ineffectiveness of Conservative opposition to Indian independence a decade later is best understood in terms of the pragmatic requirements of a party in opposition. Even after 1945 there was still a will to resist Indian independence: purportedly liberal figures within the party, including Macmillan and R.A.B. Butler, were dismayed by what they regarded as a moral failure, while the future tribune of the right, Enoch Powell, busied himself with plans to recolonise India with British administrators. As Owen demonstrates, it was Churchill, the erstwhile leader of the 1930s rebels, who calculated that there was no political advantage in resisting the inevitable. In the full expectation that his dire predictions would come true, Churchill resigned himself and his party to Indian independence [88].

Whereas opposition to Indian independence in the 1930s and 1940s and support for white settlers in Rhodesia in the 1960s and 1970s became, to some degree, popular causes, the defence of Britain's Middle East bastions in Suez, Cyprus and Aden was largely a concern of the Conservative Party in Parliament. As Onslow explains, it was the decision of the Iranian Prime Minister, Muhammad Mossadegh, to nationalise the assets of the Anglo-Iranian Oil Company (AIOC) in 1951 which sparked Conservative MPs into action. The AIOC refinery at Abadan was Britain's largest overseas investment and the apparent inability of the British government to defend these corporate assets rekindled the imperial instincts of the party, four years after the exit from India. Onslow suggests that the British government's cautious response to the nationalisation of the AIOC facility 'served as a key formative experience for the Suez Group and provided "the preparatory exercise" in the Conservative Party's future relations with Egypt as it helped identify people who cared about the Middle East and who worried about the appeasement of Middle East radicalism' [85: 21].

Although Western interests in Iran were largely restored as a consequence of the Western-backed coup against Mossadegh in 1953, by this time Conservative backbenchers had turned their attention to Britain's largest overseas military facility at Suez in Egypt. After its first meeting, on 5 October 1953, the Suez Group established itself as a 'well organised faction' of a kind which was highly unusual in the Conservative Party. Onslow argues that the group was more representative and more influential than its reputation as a rag-bag assortment of reactionary mavericks might suggest. Many of its members were progressive on domestic issues, and behind its leaders, Charles Waterhouse and Julian Amery, were numerous figures of past and future influence, including a former Chairman, Ralph Assheton, and a future Cabinet minister, Enoch Powell. During the Anglo-Egyptian negotiations over the evacuation of the base, the party's whips 'paid close attention to the Suez Group's activities and cultivated their contacts with the dissidents'. The activities of Waterhouse's followers provoked a reaction from those more sympathetic to colonial nationalism that would have ramifications after the outbreak of conflict with Egypt on the night of 31 October 1956. Onslow suggests that Eden's decision to abandon the invasion of Egypt a week later was influenced by the much less formalised anti-Suez group of backbenchers who objected to the government's resort to war. She states, 'The Whips' Office was acutely aware that the Government did not enjoy a massive majority and of the likely impact of a public split in the British ruling party upon international and Egyptian opinion' [86: 217].

The ostensible reason for Eden's resignation in the aftermath of the Suez war was his declining health but the influence of imperial sentiment on this seminal moment in post-war British political history is still not yet fully appreciated. The episode is worth exploring as an example of the way accumulating primary evidence, from memoirs, private papers and official documents, takes time to be assimilated into the historiography. Many in the Conservative Party, including members of the Cabinet, favoured a policy of continued assertiveness in relations with Egypt and regarded the Suez defeat as evidence of Eden's pusillanimity rather than a lesson in the futility of imperial adventurism. In the months after the war they resisted proposals to withdraw the British invasion force from Egypt and to pay dues to the newly nationalised Egyptian company. Only John Ramsden has flagged up the emergence of an anti-Eden faction consisting of Peter Thorneycroft, James Stuart, Selwyn Lloyd and David Eccles, the existence of which is evident from a scrawled note in the private papers of the Chief Whip, Patrick Buchan-Hepburn[4] [90]. Of this group of Cabinet members, Thorneycroft, Stuart and Eccles were sceptical about the ceasefire and opposed concessions to Egypt. Stuart outlined the connections between their uncompromising approach to Nasser and internal opposition to Eden in his rarely cited memoirs:

> the breaking point came when the PM announced suddenly that our forces and the French were to be withdrawn forthwith. We were only part of the way down the Canal and could have gone on to Suez without trouble. I did not object to our going IN; what I did object to was our coming OUT. I had to tell the PM of this privately and did so in no uncertain terms.[5]

The unexpurgated Cabinet minutes, which were only released in 2006, also reveal that Thorneycroft advised on the day of the ceasefire that they ought to 'Get max. force ashore at Port Said and then stand firm' and that on 27 November he opposed proposals to withdraw British forces.[6] A day earlier, Eccles had publicly aired the hardliners' terms in a speech at Malmesbury. Newspaper reports of his intervention alarmed other ministers because the preconditions Eccles presented for military evacuation were wholly unrealistic. They had to be disavowed when the withdrawal was announced on 6 December. Opposition to the payment of dues to the nationalised company continued to flourish on the backbenches after Eden's resignation and in May 1957 eight Conservative MPs resigned the party whip over the issue. This kind of material suggests that Onslow's analysis could be updated and extended by considering the ideological affinities and overlaps in personnel between the opponents of compromise in 1956–1957 and those Conservatives who later agitated for the retention of the base-colonies of Cyprus, Aden and Singapore.

Cultures of Britishness

Whereas accounts of parliamentary controversies such as that which accompanied the Suez crisis rarely discuss issues of race and gender, these concepts have become central to discussion of national identity at the end of empire. Studies of Britishness and empire have been carried forth on a rising scholarly tide in recent years and the almost irresistible flow of books and articles on this topic has been fed by two traditions which began as small historio-graphical streams in the 1980s and 1990s. The first has been concerned with the ideology of the white diaspora and relations between those who identified themselves as Britons across the world; the second has focused on the hybrid culture which emerged from British encroachments in Asia, Africa and the Americas and shaped modern notions of national identity. James Belich may be taken as a representative pioneer in the first tradition. His work on the history of New Zealand, which examined the consolidation of ties between white settlers and their metropolitan cousins, empha-sised the potency of the notion of 'better Britains' overseas [18]. A series of essay collections about the concept of British identity in the diaspora, under the editorships of Bridge and Fedorowich in 2003, Buckner and Francis in 2005, Bickers in 2010 and Thompson and Fedorowich in 2013, have explored similar themes [123; 124; 125; 153]. From featuring in specialist articles, these notions are now being incorporated into larger, synthetic accounts, most notably John Darwin's *The Empire Project*, which took a global Britannic nationalism to be one of the features which emboldened and sustained British imperialism, and Belich's own *Replenishing the Earth*, which examines the fortunes of the Anglo World commu-nity, during the years of explosive colonisation in the first decades of the 19th century and the period of recolonisation at the end of that century [4; 121].

The work of Carl Watts, Bill Schwarz and Donal Lowry on the Rhodesian UDI reveals the operations of this new historiography when applied to the last years of empire. Watts is the least interested in settler colonialism as a distinct phenomenon but he notes that had the Wilson government opted for military intervention against the Smith government after it declared UDI in 1965, they would have discovered that some senior officers in the British army were reluctant to fight a war against 'kith and kin'. With another general election pending Wilson was 'sensitive to public opinion' and recognised that many voters viewed the white Rhodesians as 'upholding Christian values, bringing civilization to Africa, and resisting the spread of Communism'. Nevertheless Watts concludes that Wilson ought to have been more effective in exploiting 'the anti-imperialist and anti-racialist trend that had been developing in Britain since the Suez crisis' [96: 409–410].

Schwarz is alive to the way in which imperial legacies remain operative even when their origins have been forgotten and his work ranges across a wider range of intellectual territory than Watts. His analysis of the last years of empire in *The White Man's World* pivots around Enoch Powell's Rivers of Blood speech in 1968 and suggests that whiteness was a kind of ideological cynosure in British culture. Powell drew from the same racial preoccupations that aroused Smith's metropolitan supporters. Schwarz cites reactions to Rhodesian UDI as an example of the ethnic populism which was a persistent feature of British culture from the late 19th century. The predisposition to sympathise with 'kith and kin' assumed that blood ties offered an assurance of common British identity. Opposition to immigration and support for Smith drew on ingrained prejudices which associated Britishness with whiteness and masculinity [114]. Shifting attention away from the metropolis and back to the periphery, Lowry suggests that for the Rhodesian settlers the issue was not just a question of skin colour. Forging their identity had entailed distinguishing their British culture from that of migrant Afrikaner labourers who were also white. Lowry quotes the view of Ethel Tawse Jollie, who had been embroiled in militant right-wing politics in Britain before migrating to Southern Rhodesia: 'The average British-born Rhodesian feels essentially that this is a British country pioneered, bought and developed by British people and he wants to keep it so' [24: 129]. Jollie's remarks raise issues about ethnicity and gender and they take on additional resonance when thinking about the second historiographical tradition which has focused attention on hybrid cultures of empire.

Perhaps the most influential figure in the second emergent tradition has been Antoinette Burton whose work on India differs in substance but has had a similar impact to Belich's on New Zealand. In *At the Heart of Empire* she examined how Indians who travelled to the imperial metropolis to study and work helped determine Victorian concepts of Englishness [99]. The agency of imperial subjects and the cultural impact of empire in the metropolis have also been key features of the ongoing Manchester University Press series *Studies in Imperialism*, whose contributors have illuminated the role of empire in shaping almost every kind of British institution, including the army and navy, medicine, museums, law and higher education, as well as drawing attention to the manner in which British and English identity has acquired specific gender and racial connotations from these intimate imperial encounters. Its editor John MacKenzie, examined the impact of imperial propaganda from the late 19th century up to 1960, but his emphasis on the significance of culture was initially taken up by historians of the 19th rather than the 20th century [109].

The chronological centre of gravity of this kind of scholarship is now shifting toward the later period; in this regard, Wendy Webster's work on Englishness and empire after 1945 may be regarded as representative. Webster deals explicitly with the culture of Englishness in recognition of 'the extent to which media representations of Britain, empire and Commonwealth were Anglocentric.' In examining the impact of visual imagery, she places particular emphasis to the gendered and spatial elements which comprise Englishness. After 1945 many women returned to a domestic environment after years of wartime work in farms and factories and this transition to the private sphere found cultural expression in the trajectory of the post-war film industry 'which increasingly expelled the home front, civilians and women'. Consequently, it was the middle- and upper-class men portrayed in *The Dam Busters, Reach for the Sky, Bridge over the River Kwai* and *Sink the Bismarck!* who became emblems of British endurance and courage in wartime. Although white women were largely excluded from the wartime epic, Webster finds that they did feature in the genre of colonial film. Cinematic portrayals of their exploits on the imperial frontier suggested that women's attempts to promote imperial reform frequently had tragic, unintended consequences. Webster argues that in films such as *Black Narcissus* and *A Town Like Alice* 'themes of British failure, humiliation and defeat are represented through females' [119: 90]. It was in their role as defenders of the home that women were celebrated in British culture. The metropolitan press depicted the real life stories of Kitty Hesselberger and Dorothy Raynes-Simpson, who repelled a Mau Mau attack on their Kenyan residence, as a triumphant defence of white domesticity against the brutalities of Africa. Such narratives were easily transposed onto debates about black immigration in which English homeliness was imperilled by the unruliness of black Caribbean migrants. On Webster's account the establishment of multi-racial households marked a moment of crisis for English domesticity. Fears about the stability of such unfamiliar arrangements were gendered; the preoccupation with the threat posed to white women by black suitors was encapsulated in the ubiquitous rhetorical question: 'Would you let your daughter marry a black man?' These trends reached a lurid conclusion in Powell's Rivers of Blood speech in which he used the purported experience of a white woman having her windows broken and excreta shoved through her letterbox by black immigrants as representative of the embattled status of the resident community in the aftermath of empire. Webster concludes that by the 1960s 'Englishness was threatened by empire, by Commonwealth, and by their legacies, not only in empire but at home' [119: 181].

The 2014 referendum on Scottish independence illustrated the extent to which the other constituent elements of the United Kingdom possess their own distinct cultures and exposed the vulnerability of English conceptions of identity to interrogation and provincialisation. Krishan Kumar has identified an old 'inner empire' which was 'the result of the Anglo-Norman conquest of Wales and Ireland and later the shotgun marriage with Scotland' [106: 307]. It has become almost a cliché to note the vigour with which the constituent ethnic parts of this inner empire took up the imperialist cause in Asia, Africa and the Americas. Kevin Kenny and John MacKenzie have edited volumes in the *Companion Series* to the *Oxford History of the British Empire* dealing with the Irish and Scottish role in the establishment, maintenance and dissolution of the British empire [105; 110]. In his historiographical survey MacKenzie validated the 'Four Nations' approach to imperial history, in part on the grounds that 'it is even possible to suggest that the relationship of various British ethnicities to a wider imperial world were, in truth, very important in the maintenance and development of identities' [13: 1246].

Lowry's analysis of Ulster and empire is pertinent to the study of decolonisation, and may be taken as representative of the historiographical trend towards examining the individual traditions of the four nations. His arguments are informed by his interest in Rhodesian history. He notes: 'Almost alone among former colonists the Rhodesians still used the failing vocabulary of Empire and the Belfast Protestant working class, in the decades following the second world war, still referred to the Sandy Row district of their city as the "heart of empire"' [108: 202]. Ian Paisley's *Protestant Telegraph* emphasised the commonality of the Rhodesian and Northern Irish experience on the grounds that both were confronted with the problem of 'primitive natives'. The Vanguard Movement of William Craig sought to ape the Rhodesian precedent by calling for its own UDI and established links with the National Front in England. This was not a Britishness of domesticity and complacency but of confrontation drawn from the colonial frontier, which clung to the monarchy as the only uncorrupted element in post-imperial Britain. Lowry concludes 'perceptions of empire came to divide nationalist and unionist identities and these perceptions lie at the very heart of the continued alienation of these traditions from each other' [108: 209].

Lowry, Schwarz and Webster are principally concerned with what can very approximately be described as a conservative culture and right-wing politics, but Stuart Ward and Jodi Burkett have found evidence of imperial transactions in the apparently more subversive trends of the 1960s. Ward argues that the supposed rebelliousness of that generation's satirists masked their ingrained conservatism. While Peter Cook's lampooning of Harold Macmillan's best patrician manner is well known, John Bird's disparaging imitations of Jomo Kenyatta have been almost forgotten. According to Ward, Cook and Bird's cultural output exhibited a shared scepticism 'about the readiness of Africa for self-government, and in particular the appropriateness of someone like Kenyatta for the role of colonial liberator' [117: 106].

The traditionalist roots of 1960s radicalism are also inspected by Burkett although her focus is on institutional politics. Her analysis of the imperial legacy examines four organisations made up predominantly of middle class activists on the British left: the

Campaign for Nuclear Disarmament (CND), the Anti-Apartheid Movement (AAM), the National Union of Students (NUS) and the Northern Ireland Civil Rights Movement (NICRM). Burkett suggests that the left found it difficult to abandon traditional elements of imperial identity even as they attempted to configure a more progressive notion of Britishness. The radicals of the 1960s 'were often outwardly anti-imperial, while relying unthinkingly on the "realities" of British superiority to articulate the world around them and their place within it' [98: 12]. For example, CND's desire to redefine British 'greatness' as a moral quality appeared to betoken an ongoing and influential role for the country in world affairs. In another context the AAM was less interested in rehashing historical accusations concerning the sins of British colonialism than in publicising the contemporary requirement to contain South African expansionism, which required an interventionist role for Britain. While itemising the historical encumbrances of the imperial past under which they laboured, Burkett also argues that, for the left, the end of empire 'offered a great opportunity to create a post-imperial Britain that was progressive and moral' [98: 196]. Although it was inhibited by its constitution from extending its reach too far beyond the realm of education policy, the NUS challenged racial discrimination in employment and housing policy because its members, many of whom identified themselves as black, required part-time jobs and accommodation. On the question of sporting sanctions against South Africa, it made unavailing efforts to persuade the Oxford and Cambridge university rugby clubs not to tour the apartheid state. In these cases the left integrated traditional notions of British liberality and fair play into an effective critique of the conservatism of domestic politics.

Burkett pays more attention to politics than to the role which an increasingly desegregated British popular culture played in advancing anti-racism in the metropolis and liberation in the periphery. The MCF, for example, accorded great significance to events such as the celebratory Africa Freedom Day concerts which, although failing to net Shirley Bassey, recruited to the liberationist cause artists such as Annie Ross and Humphrey Lyttelton, the nephew of Churchill's reactionary Colonial Secretary, Oliver Lyttelton. They became a regular May event at the Royal Festival Hall during the 1960s.[7] Mention of the Royal Festival Hall brings us to a final discussion of the presence and absence of imperialism in the metropolis and the controversy over whether the former is more significant than the latter. The imperial context in which the Festival of Britain took place had largely been ignored in the historiography until Becky Conekin devoted a chapter of her book on the subject to the empire as 'the place that was almost absent' from this display of British enterprise and endeavour [101: 183–202]. Jo Littler subsequently extended Conekin's analysis by arguing that this apparent absenteeism served as camouflage for the imperialist discourse employed during the festival. In designing the festival's iconic image, Abram Games offered a modernist rendering of Britannia, which masked what were otherwise pronounced associations with old-fashioned imperial ambition and overseas conquest. Littler also unpicks themes of neo-imperial mastery, Commonwealth benevolence and insular parochialism in the festival's exhibits. In this vein, the prominence of scientific discovery during the festival, including coverage of future space exploration, may be interpreted as a new means of articulating the expansiveness of British ambitions, transposed from an earthly to a celestial realm. Summing up the message of the festival, Littler argues that Britain was portrayed as 'a nation which is small at home but therefore all the more impressive for its imperial legacy and benevolence' [107: 37].

Five years after the Festival of Britain and one day after the end of the Suez war a statue of Jan Smuts was unveiled in Parliament Square. To the present generation he is one of the least recognisable of the legendary figures represented in the square but Schwarz suggests that the mishaps and controversies which accompanied the decision to fashion an image of Smuts illustrates the way in which imperial themes were understood in the era of decolonisation. According to Schwarz, at his death in 1950 Smuts was 'more visible than any other colonial statesman and more prominent than many domestic politicians'. Although he was a 'man of the frontier', he played a decisive role in shaping debates about Britishness. Schwarz states,

> Smuts struggled to reconcile his faith in the supremacy of white civilization with a genuine regard for liberty and democracy. ... he bequeathed to the British a discourse on race which could be recuperated by post-war domestic politicians when called upon to have something intelligent or acceptable to say on the issues of empire and immigration.

The most ardent defender of his reputation during parliamentary discussions of memorial plans was the Conservative MP, Charles Doughty, who was also a militant critic of the anti-racist stance of Fenner Brockway and the MCF. Schwarz notes that the selection of Epstein as the sculptor of the Smuts statue was somewhat incongruous given that, like many modernists, he had been influenced by black art traditions. Finally, the perfunctory coverage of the unveiling itself, Schwarz argues, illustrated the uneasy relationship of mid-1950s Britain with the legacy of imperialism: 'The monumental narrative that in earlier decades had seemed the natural mode of representing imperial Britain no longer carried the same authority' [115: 202–203]. Despite evidence of diminishing British confidence at the end of empire, the legacy of Smuts as 'a philosopher of race' endured and his white supremacism became embedded in the ethnic populism of the metropolis [114].

The question of how much significance should be accorded to events such as the Festival of Britain and cultural objects such as the Smuts statue continues to be controversial. The extent to which cultural discourse matters is the principal area of contestation between traditional historians of empire and proponents of postcolonial methods. Writing at the start of the new millennium, Ward set the contributors to his edited volume, *British Culture and the End of Empire* in opposition to a 'minimal impact thesis', espoused by such luminaries as Bernard Porter, David Cannadine, Kenneth Morgan, Arthur Marwick, A.J.P. Taylor, George Boyce and Max Beloff [118: 5]. Some of Ward's nominees were dead and others did not seem particularly committed to the minimalist cause, but one, Bernard Porter, did take up Ward's challenge. He offered a full defence of the thesis that British politics and culture were largely insulated from imperial influence in *The Absent-Minded Imperialists*; Andrew Thompson, on the other hand, retailed a more nuanced and moderate form of scepticism in *The Empire Strikes Back?* [111; 116]. Porter deals principally with the 19th and early 20th century and contrasts the substantial material impact of empire with its highly attenuated cultural legacy. He concludes that by the 1960s 'Britain was very much more than an imperial power ... just as she had been more than an imperial power before then; national policies and characteristics had "other roots entirely" and the most significant of these was the "free-market capitalist economic system"' [111: 301–302]. Defenders of the postcolonial approach charged Porter with methodological naivety. 'Rich in evidence but weak in interpretive power' was Burton's pithy summary [100]. When Porter returned to the fray, he attributed much of the criticism to the misplaced belief that he was an apologist for empire and ruefully noted that Thompson had pursued similar themes without provoking such a backlash [112].

Thompson also questioned the excesses of the maximal impact school by disaggregating their larger claims in order to itemise the significance of imperial transactions in different places and at different times. On the question of British identity formation, Thompson acknowledges that an exclusive imperial focus might lead to a neglect of other influences emanating either from the United States or Europe. But in contrast to Porter, he cautions against the use of polling data, which appeared to demonstrate popular ignorance of empire in mid-20th century Britain, to support the notion that decolonisation went almost unnoticed. News of the Suez war, the Mau Mau conflict and the emergency in Nyasaland resonated in the metropolis. Furthermore although Thompson rejects Tabili's notion that British attitudes to immigration were wholly determined by the circumstances of empire, he acknowledges that the colonial experience must be integrated, alongside local factors, into an explanation of British policy in this area. Most significantly of all, *The Empire Strikes Back?* suggests that ongoing debates about Britishness are still informed by differing interpretations of imperial history which have penetrated down to the popular level. The prevalence of imperial themes in British museum exhibitions and in debates about multi-culturalism, give a strong indication that matters of empire need to be recognised when thinking about national identity [116].

Conclusions

Although the lack of prominence given to empire in British general elections may still blind historians of the Conservative and Labour parties to the significance of the subject, students of 20th century party politics ought to be cognisant of the emerging literature on party politics and decolonisation. The work of Howe, Owen, Morgan, Murphy, Muldoon and Onslow is marked by scepticism about large claims regarding the transactions between domestic and imperial politics yet they have demonstrated that the affairs of the periphery left a significant impression on debates within and between the parties [72; 81; 82; 84; 86; 87]. They also provide a foundation on which future historians can build: it would be fascinating to investigate the continuities and discontinuities between Churchill's campaign against the Government of India Act and the efforts of his son-in-law, Duncan Sandys, to harry Wilson over the Rhodesia issue 30 years later. If the historiographical problem with the high politics of decolonisation is its lack of integration into domestic political history, then the difficulty which arises in examining the cultural imprint of empire in the metropolis is that it is tied to almost intractable and always controversial questions about British and English identity. Although most British residents are likely to encounter regular evidence of the imperial legacy in architecture, cuisine, sport, music, literature and fashion, for historians there is a difficulty in establishing whether these markers are signs of a society complicit in imperial adventurism and a culture inextricably bound to the assertion of British superiority in Africa, Asia and the Americas, or whether the establishment, maintenance and dissolution of empire was a narrower project of interest and significance to particular sectors of British society and politics. Advocates of postcolonial methods have turned to an analysis of culture as a point of entry into these debates, and their attempt to destabilise the conceptual boundaries fencing off metropolis from periphery has achieved some notable successes in examining the late imperial period. There is scope for further synthetic work in, for example, connecting Ward's analysis of the conservatism of the cultural rebellion of the 1960s to Burkett's analysis of the nostalgic elements in the left's political platform. Yet Porter and Thompson are right to emphasise that some of the larger claims need disaggregating and that non-imperial influences on notions of Britishness must also be acknowledged [111; 116]. Thompson's discussion of multi-culturalism raises salient questions, which may have been nagging at attentive readers, regarding the nature of black British identity. Consideration of these matters requires some engagement with a wider literature about the role of migration in the transformation and decline of British imperialism.

3 Migration

The study of migration offers an opportunity to consider how changes which occurred in the last years of the British Empire affected the lives of ordinary people and it would be an inattentive historian who overlooked the conspicuous and compelling role that migration has played in the development of public history in Britain. There are a variety of practical, theoretical and even reputational reasons why those people who participated in, or endured, voluntary or coerced relocation during the era of British decolonisation make attractive subjects for historians. The most mundane of these is that many of the migrants are still alive and willing to tell their stories; and in places like London, Birmingham, Leicester and Bradford they share the city with universities. Yet geographical proximity is not the determining consideration because for many years such migrant communities were ignored by historians. More recently the study of people on the move has been given impetus, first by the injunction to write 'history from below', then by the requirement for inter-disciplinarity and currently by the emphasis on transnationalism. Such investigations also dovetail neatly with the 'impact agenda' of the Arts and Humanities Research Council (AHRC) and the Research Excellence Framework (REF), which require scholars to demonstrate that their work resonates outside of academia.

Retailing migrant stories to a wider public forms only part of the historiographical picture because we are also in the midst of a consuming and contested national and local debate about British immigration policy. Such discussions often exhibit a wearying lack of historical perspective, particularly with regard to the decisive role which the British state has played in shaping the demography of both metropolis and periphery. The study of migration ought to be conditioned by an awareness of the responsibility of governments which have sometimes forced people to uproot their lives, sometimes offered sanctuary, sometimes facilitating migration and sometimes prevented relocation. For example, commitment to the free movement of people inside the empire became a key component of imperial ideology and was embodied in legislation, including the Empire Settlement Act of 1922, which incentivised migration to the dominions, and the British Nationality Act of 1948, which gave expression to the notion of a common imperial nationality. The final abandonment of assisted migration in the 1970s and the passing of increasingly restrictive immigration legislation after 1962 were significant markers of imperial decline. Beyond the legislative sphere, action or inaction by the imperial executive also left a substantial legacy. The failure to prepare adequately for the mass movement of people which occurred during the partition of India contributed to the greatest human disaster of the era of decolonisation, while the ejection of the population of the Chagos Islands led to tragedy on a smaller scale. As we shall see a new historiography about the former and ongoing political controversy about the latter illustrate the resonance of the imperial past in the post-imperial present. Before turning to these movements around the periphery of empire, it is appropriate to investigate the growing literature on the experience of migration to and from Britain.

Migration between metropolis and periphery

The disembarkation from *Empire Windrush* at Tilbury of approximately 500 Caribbean migrants in 1948 has become emblematic of the transformations brought about by the relocation of people from the imperial periphery to the metropolis. Aside from the political controversies it stirred, one of the reasons why the *Windrush* generation have achieved prominence in post-war British history is that their descendants have recorded their experiences for posterity. A book and television series, simply entitled *Windrush*, by Mike and Trevor Phillips, who are the sons of first generation Guianese migrants, was published to coincide with the 50th anniversary of the ship's arrival. A video recording of the programme can still be watched on Youtube. Scrutiny of the book gives a sense of the possibilities and potential pitfalls which arise when authors use oral history techniques to describe the past of their

own community. Such insider histories may, for the defensive purpose of demonstrating migrant achievement, offer an edifying but
not necessarily representative portrayal. The tendency in *Windrush*
is to push class divisions within the West Indian community to
one side and to marginalise the significance of conflicts between
different migrant groups in order to emphasise the endurance of
the first generation and their contribution to the host society. The
list of interviewees who spoke to the authors is full of ex-service
personnel, magistrates, councillors and professionals with a supplementary infusion of successful artists and entertainers, such as
Lenny Henry, Lynton Kwesi Johnson and Jazzie B. Even those figures whose stories are less wholesome, such as Johnny Edgecombe,
the termination of whose affair with Christine Keeler kickstarted
the Profumo affair, are representative of a certain glamorous
notoriety rather than the mundanities of low wage labour for the
first generation of migrants from the Caribbean and unemployment for many of the second [146].

There are countervailing advantages to such insider accounts. They
are based on an intimate knowledge of the lives described that is
unavailable to outsiders. When, in their postscript, the Phillips brothers
consider the legacy of their parents as representatives of the migrant
experience, they portray them as part of a generation who 'walked
the streets looking for shelter, or worked through the night for years
at a stretch'; they also write directly to the next generation of their
own experiences as the black children of migrants in a predominantly
white society. *Windrush* provides an authentic sense of the social texture of Britain as experienced by African-Caribbean migrants and
identifies some under-represented events in the history of black
Britain. For example, most historians of the 1980s are oblivious to
the Black People's Day of Action on 2 March 1981 and the description
of the campaign by the people involved in its genesis and organisation provides a necessary corrective. The marchers protested about
the inadequate institutional response to the deaths of 13 young black
people in the Deptford Fire. A sister of one of those who died recalled:

> I never realised how many people actually was in support of us until
> I saw them all scaling these fences, basically and joining in the
> march, and that was touching, because you never really see your peers
> as being real interested in things like that. That's sort of a big people
> thing. [146: 340]

Outsider accounts are afflicted with a set of methodological problems different from those evident in *Windrush*. As a white academic visiting the Caribbean from the United States to speak to return migrants, George Gmelch was conscious that his outsider status affected the outcome of his work. When collecting his oral histories, he intuited that some of his interviewees were reticent on the subject of the racial hostility they experienced in Britain and the United States. Certainly, there is a marked contrast between the emphasis given to the prejudice experienced in Britain by the people who spoke to the Phillips brothers and the often gratifying accounts about the 'friendly attitude of the people in Lancashire' or 'the salt of the earth' character of the citizens of Newcastle, mentioned by Gmelch's subjects. Given the lack of legal protection available to the migrants prior to the introduction of anti-discrimination legislation by Wilson's Labour government in 1965 and the widespread ignorance and fear generated by press coverage of the migrants' arrival, Gmelch is probably correct to conclude that his status inhibited discussion of some of these more painful subjects. Although he interviewed many fewer people than Phillips and Phillips and spoke only to those from Barbados, his work takes greater account of the experience of migrants in the British provinces. It is useful to recall that Barbadian migrants could be found working as butchers in Letchworth, as prison nurses in Holloway and as art students in Newcastle. It was often through such labour that they established some sense of fellowship both with other migrants and with the host community. Gmelch comments: 'If there was a dominant theme in these narratives, it is work. It is difficult to overstate how hard these individuals worked.' Most significantly of all, his focus on return migrants demonstrates the ambiguous nature of their engagement with notions of postcolonial identity. For Gmelch's subjects, forging a new black British identity was less of a priority than re-engaging with their Caribbean roots. He argues: 'Even after living many years abroad and successfully adjusting to English or North American society the orientation of the migrants was always toward the Caribbean' [136: 71].

The decisive moment for those black migrants who stayed in Britain and for their children was Enoch Powell's 1968 speech predicting 'rivers of blood' which exposed the virulent racial hostility of the host community. Phillips and Phillips suggest: 'After

Powell the different Caribbean communities had been completely racialised and radicalised, welded together into a single black community by the heat of the political passions he ignited' [146: 254]. A new generation of intellectuals with roots in the Caribbean reacted against the cultural belittlement and explicit racial hostility revealed during the Powellite moment. As the 50th anniversary of the speech approaches, the impact of figures such as Stuart Hall, Paul Gilroy and Darcus Howe on debates about postcolonial British identity offer a compelling subject for historicisation. Gilroy continues to offer sharp observations on current race relations, such as on the subject of David Cameron's attack on British multi-culturalism at Munich in 2011. Just before his death in 2014, Hall was the subject of an elegiac cinematic tribute by the director John Akomfrah and an intellectual biography of Howe by Robin Bunce and Paul Field appeared in 2013 [69; 103]. The apparently new currents in post-war British intellectual history represented by Gilroy, Hall and Howe, require some greater contextualisation in terms of the longer history of black migration to Britain, which encompasses the story of migrants from Africa and Asia.

The literature about earlier generations of migrants indicates that class played a decisive role in the entrenchment of Britishness among the black population of the empire. Anne Spry Rush notes that long before the journey of the *Windrush*, the middle classes of the Anglophone Caribbean 'used their understanding of Britishness to establish a place for themselves in the British imperial world and thus to negotiate the challenges of decolonization' [113: 1]. When paternalist officials attempted to revise the traditional and very rigid Anglocentric education curriculum which prevailed in the Caribbean, parents protested on the grounds that a knowledge of British culture and history was precisely what their children needed if they were to better their status in a society dominated by those traditions. On Rush's account migrants to the metropolis employed their mastery over the protocols of Britishness to achieve advancement. Harold Moody established the League of Coloured Peoples in 1931 in order to moderate the hostility of white Britons through the medium of 'scholarly lectures, tennis parties, garden parties and cricket matches'. Rush argues that Moody's goal was to subvert the Little England mentality, which was inclusive of different classes but racially exclusive, and assert instead a bourgeois notion of Britishness which would entitle black migrants to acceptance, on condition that they conformed to the protocols of middle class respectability [113].

In her account of the experiences of black British seamen, Laura Tabili explores a different aspect of the intersection between class and race in inter-war Britain. She argues that black seamen who had taken up residence in Britain were victimised as a consequence of the extension of exploitative employment practices by the imperial shipping companies. This took legal form in the notorious Coloured Alien Seamen Order of 1925 which forced black British subjects living in the metropolis to register as aliens if they did not have passports, which very few did. The order was used to intimidate and harass black residents of Bristol, Liverpool and other port cities. Proletarian black seamen resisted repatriation and instead asserted a form of Britishness informed by notions of justice and liberality [256]. Winston James extends this analysis to argue that these inter-war residents and the new generation of migrants who arrived after 1948 were both caught between the two logics of imperialism, one of which applied to the periphery and the other to the metropolis. In the Caribbean 'black people had been taught that they were British and came to think of themselves as such'; but on arrival in the metropolis they encountered the logic of 'a white man's country' [104: 377]. According to James it is this metropolitan logic which connects the white riots in the port cities of 1919 to the almost uniform system of racial discrimination in housing and employment in mid-century Britain and to the institutionalised racism revealed by the botched investigation into the murder of Stephen Lawrence by white racists in Eltham in 1993. In response, many migrant families rejected the hierarchical class systems and parochial rivalries of the Caribbean in order to unite under a West Indian identity, whose most prominent representatives were a cricket team capable of repeatedly defeating England [104].

This literature on Caribbean migrants demonstrates the influence that apparently abstract concepts of race and identity exerted on changing practices of exclusion and inclusion during the era of decolonisation; that this relationship applied more widely is illustrated by the less closely scrutinised case of the refugees from Uganda who relocated to Britain in the early 1970s. The Ugandan coup which Idi Amin orchestrated in 1971 was initially registered as a gratifying development by British diplomats and expatriates who were disillusioned with the leftist inclination of his predecessor, Milton Obote. After a brief period of optimism, relations with Amin's regime deteriorated and reached a nadir when, on 5 August 1972, he announced that the country's Asian residents would be expelled within 90 days. The intriguing nature of the primary source material and lack of secondary commentary about this topic was brought to my attention by an undergraduate student whose dissertation examined the influence of domestic political pressures upon the Heath government's handling of the crisis. At independence in 1962 approximately half of the Asians living in Uganda had chosen to retain their status as Citizens of the UK and Colonies but their right of entry to Britain was jeopardised by the restrictive Commonwealth Immigrants Act of 1968 and by domestic political hostility.

The Prime Minister's files at the National Archives are an obvious but underutilised starting point for examination of these issues, and what they reveal is the trepidation which Heath and his ministers felt in the midst of the backlash against immigration which Powell had initiated. The Chief Whip, Francis Pym, described the affair as 'a very dangerous political crisis' and suggested that further efforts to accommodate the refugees risked 'prejudicing existing immigrants'. When the migrants from Uganda arrived, the Environment Secretary, Peter Walker, complained that officials had allowed 'local opposition to build up without the calming influence of local PR'. Heath himself insisted that although Ugandans with British passports would have to be granted entry 'we will *not* accept a *single one of the others*'.[1] This kind of material is consonant with Yumiko Hamai's recent analysis of press coverage which suggests that the somewhat complacent self-congratulation, evident in Heath's memoirs and elsewhere, at Britain's decision to permit entry to the refugees is unwarranted. A series of media panics over Caribbean, Pakistani and Kenyan migration established the context for press coverage of Amin's expulsion decree: on the one hand, the *Daily Express* fulminated against a potential invasion of Britain by non-patrial Asians, while on the other, more liberal commentators urged compassion for those fleeing Uganda. Although the latter succeeded in eliciting some sympathy for Amin's victims, Hamai asserts that public debates about the Ugandan migrants took no account of legacy of imperialism in setting the context for the crisis or the international legal requirement to accept British citizens once they had been expelled from their country of residence [137].

Later media coverage of the Ugandan expellees tends to tell an edifying story of economic success but recent interpretations by Emma Robertson and Joanna Herbert have modified this interpretation both with regard to the migrants' willingness to accept the terms presented to them for their integration and in generating a more nuanced picture of their material fortunes. As this work demonstrates, oral histories of migration need not be employed purely for the defensive purposes of reassuring the host society. In an approach which is often reserved for reputedly great figures of politics and culture, Robertson focuses on the life of a single individual migrant and seeks to contextualise it within imperial history. She argues that the story of her interviewee, Julie, 'needs to be understood in the context of British imperialism and its post-war demise' [147: 260]. Julie spent her childhood in Southern Rhodesia and resettled in Uganda following her marriage. After occupying an intermediate layer between blacks and whites in what Robertson describes as the 'useful racial hierarchy' of colonialism, her family abandoned their business assets and personal possessions when they fled to Britain as a consequence of Amin's decree. She was one of a small number of expellees who settled in York and found work at the Rowntree confectionery factory. In subjective terms Robertson emphasises some of Julie's positive emotions, including the sense of communal affiliation with other female workers at the factory, but she also describes her resistance to the agenda of integration set by the British government. This was particularly evident in her determination to establish links with other Asian Muslim families, which was a more exacting task in York than it would have been in Bradford or Leeds [147].

In cautioning against generalisation and emphasising the specificity of particular life experiences, Robertson's work overlaps with that of Herbert who examined the fortunes of migrants in Leicester and London while working at universities in those cities. Whereas Robertson contextualises the biography of one migrant, Herbert synthesises contributions from 70 interviewees, and utilises extant oral history archives in the two cities. In conceptual terms she situates her work within the expanding literature on diasporic identities and argues for an alternative narrative about the refugees: 'one that neither bemoans their attachments to India nor celebrates their loyalty to Britain but explores how Ugandan Asians developed more complex transnational affiliations to both Uganda and Britain'. Memories recalled by the interviewees suggest an attachment to the African outdoors, and this raises questions about the notion of home as a comfortable interior space. Having explored some of the gender influences on the migrant experience, and particularly notions of masculinity and entrepreneurial success, Herbert indicates that the class positioning of the migrants is not as straightforward as might appear from their portrayal as an ascendant middle-class success story. Their ensnarement in a series of bureaucratic obstacles during the process of uprooting engendered doubts among the expellees about their reception in Britain. Having lost their possessions many undertook manual labour before reorienting themselves to the British commercial environment. The Indian government had disavowed its connections to the Asian communities in East Africa and many of the migrants were effectively estranged from the Indian or Asian identities which tended to be thrust upon them in Britain. In terms of memorialisation, Herbert records a widespread feeling that they wanted their contribution to the development of Uganda to be recognised [141].

A decade after the arrival of the Ugandan expellees, the Thatcher government redefined British citizenship to exclude most residents of the former empire. This was the culmination of a period of tightening legal restrictions on Commonwealth immigration and the question of whether this was necessary to mollify public hostility is one of the most contentious in the historiography. The initial orthodoxy, cogently expressed in the policy-oriented work of Nicholas Deakin of the Institute of Race Relations (IRR), was that a paternalist class of ministers and officials had, with partial success, grappled with the social problems which accompanied immigration, including popular resistance to the presence of the migrants [70]. Such ideas found their way into a popular history of immigration, sponsored by Channel 4 in the 1980s, which stated: 'It would be quite wrong to claim that the politicization of race was solely (or even largely) the result of politicians' actions and words ... public opinion, as expressed through local pressure groups, began to exert a powerful anti-immigrant (and often overtly racist) influence over local MPs' [155: 132]. One American political scientist, Anthony Messina, went further and argued that until the mid-1970s, the leaders of Britain's political parties had colluded in an attempt to depoliticise race relations and that the Powellite revolt was an expression of popular discontent with this comfortable elitist consensus [79]. Precisely the opposite conclusions were drawn by a new generation of radical scholars, working at the IRR and publishing their revisionist studies in the journal *Race & Class*. Ambalavaner Sivanandan, argued that both the initial liberality and the later restrictionism of British immigration law were determined by the demands made on labour by capital [92]. Rather than hostile attitudes being transmitted upwards from the host society, racist presuppositions, on Sivanandan's account, percolated downwards from the social and political elite, whose administration of empire had been predicated on notions of ineradicable racial hierarchies.

It was not until 1997 that a fully historicised statement of the revisionist case was articulated, with the publication of books by Ian R. G. Spencer and Kathleen Paul. In his conclusion to *British Immigration Policy Since 1939*, Spencer argued that the notion of a liberal elite class holding back popular unrest was an illusion. He stated 'the approach of Britain's policy makers was always racialised' and concluded that official discourse about immigration rested on an unquestioned assumption 'that "coloured" immigrants in large numbers could not be assimilated' [150: 153]. Paul's brand of revisionism was punchier than Spencer's, as is evident from the title of her monograph, *Whitewashing Britain*. Her examination of the relationship between race, citizenship and immigration led her to conclude that skin colour 'had the most direct and immediate effect on concepts of British nationality' [145: xii]. Only once this is acknowledged, Paul argues, does it become possible to resolve the apparent inconsistencies of British immigration policy. Why for example, did British governments fund migration by white Britons to the Commonwealth during an era that was punctuated by financial crises and labour shortages? Why did the Ministry of Labour look to aliens from white continental Europe as a potential source of new British citizens, while discouraging existing black British subjects living in the imperial periphery from entering the country?

On Paul's account the racial attitudes of Britain's political and social elites offer the most plausible answers to these questions. Migrants to Australia, Canada and Rhodesia were spurred on by the state, because they were from the 'restricted community of white-skinned British stock' and could thus be relied upon to defend British values overseas [145: 43]. In order to resolve the labour shortages which were exacerbated by this loss of 'British stock' to the Commonwealth, post-war governments encouraged immigration from eastern Europe. Despite their legal status as aliens, these European migrants were plausible candidates for integration and were thus preferred to non-white British citizens from the empire whose blackness was regarded as a bar to effective assimilation. Lastly, Irish migrants were in an intermediary position: white and therefore sufficiently similar to be allowed entry, but with cultural habits which were sufficiently different to generate unease. Paul demonstrates the prevalence of the concept of 'British stock' in mid-century political debates but encounters greater difficulty in tracing the influence of racial concepts when examining minister-ial and official records which are written in the carefully coded language of the British bureaucracy. She suggests that the Working Party established in 1948 to investigate labour recruitment from the colonies registered non-white immigration as a threat to the social order but acknowledges that there were dissenting voices and that some non-white female labour was employed in the early years of the National Health Service. There were also differences between the relative liberality of the Conservative Home Secretary, David Maxwell Fyffe, on immigration issues and the restrictive instincts of his successor, Gwilym Lloyd George. In acknowledging these nuances and qualifications, Paul attests to disagreements between elites regarding the supposed dangers which colonial immigrants posed to British society and this is a theme taken up by those who have criticised the revisionist approach [145].

Behind the bland title of Randall Hansen's *Citizenship and Immigration in Post-War Britain* lurks an author bursting with indig-nation. Expectations that post-revisionist work will be marked by a temperate reconciliation between orthodoxy and revisionism are confounded by Hansen's tone of histrionic reasonableness. He argues that the historiographical rot set in with the politically motivated argument of Sivanandan and others, which suggested that the racial proclivities of political elites regulated the British discourse on immigration, and responds in the register of high-handed dismissal: 'the thesis appears so simply deterministic as not to merit attention' [140: 12]. Paul's later analysis is, on Hansen's account, 'not merely untenable, it is, as the archives on which she bases her hypothesis make clear, wholly untenable' [140: 246]. This polemical approach generates some puzzles of its own. For example, Hansen asserts that the notion of elite responsibility for the racialisation of immigration debates is 'logically incoherent'; but his counter-argument, that the public was already predisposed to resist non-white immigration, rests on the uncovering of empirical counter-example rather than the identification of logical fallacies in Paul's thesis. There is also a measure of inconsistency in asserting that the work of the racialisation theorists cannot be defended with reference to government documents, while acknowledging that the arguments which the Marquess of Salisbury made in Cabinet for immigration controls during the 1950s 'appear to derive from colour alone' [140: 70]. Remarks attributed to Salisbury in the notebooks of the Cabinet Secretary, Norman Brook, to which neither Paul nor Hansen had access, amplify the racist language employed during these discussions. Adopting eugenicist rhetoric Salisbury stated at Cabinet that what he found troubling about immigration was its 'Effect on racial characteristics of [the] English people in [the] long run'.[2] Despite his protestations to the contrary, Hansen's disagreement with the revisionists actually pivots on matters of interpretation and more specifically on the question of whether such outpourings of racial feeling were relatively uncommon at a time when a liberal approach to immigration had many defenders inside government. In emphasising the influence exerted by opponents of immigration controls, Hansen offers effective correction to the uniform picture presented in some revisionist literature. In particular he locates the debate about immigration within a broader policy-making context about decolonisation and demonstrates the manner in which the anti-restrictionist Colonial Office were able to fend off the demand for controls until 1962. The merger of the Colonial Office and Commonwealth Relations Office in 1966 and the absorption of both by the Foreign Office two years later was a key institutional development which facilitated the increasingly illiberal acts of 1968 and 1971 [140].

Beyond the polemicizing, Paul and Hansen concur on some points. They offer congruent views of the British Nationality Act of 1948 which established a common citizenship for British subjects whether they resided in the imperial metropolis or periphery. Despite its apparent liberality, Paul and particularly Hansen emphasise that the act was not intended to facilitate large scale migration from the colonies to Britain; it was rather a defensive measure taken at a time when notions of imperial identity were imperilled by the emergence of new citizenship laws in the former dominions, most notably Canada. As Carter suggested in his review of *Citizenship and Immigration* 'Hansen's own case is not always as contrary to the racialisation thesis as he likes to claim' [127]. At one point Hansen more or less concedes that debates about immigration were influenced by racial hierarchies and states: 'it would be naive to claim that policy-makers in the 1950s were unaffected by imperialist assumptions of European superiority' [140: 63]. It is in the realm of policy rather than norms, that Hansen makes some telling criticisms of the revisionists, whose theories cannot, he asserts, account for the liberal legislative framework which was maintained until 1962. His suggestion that there was no need, or rationale, for the downward transmission of racist attitudes from policymakers to the masses is persuasive. The least convincing passages in *Whitewashing Britain* are those which suggest that reliable opinion poll data demonstrating popular hostility towards non-white migration only emerged after the disorders of 1958 and that it would be 'presumptuous' to project these backwards into the early 1950s. Cesarani notes that Paul ignored 'the considerable evidence of spontaneous colour bars and popular racism', while conceding her point that officials were making plans for restrictions independently and in advance of any popular demands [128].

A number of the interpretive disagreements between Paul and Hansen are a consequence of either the manner in which debates are framed or the employment of different kinds of source material. It is on this point that the nature of the documentation becomes a critical question. Spencer, Hansen and Paul all examine the minutes and memoranda of the Cabinet Office; anybody familiar with the bureaucratic register in which these are written will recognise the contrast between the contentious subject matter and the blandness of the form in which these discussions are recorded [140; 145; 150]. Hansen concentrates on arguments between ministers about the need for legislative action. By contrast, Paul and Spencer range more broadly in order to examine how the Ministry of Labour and the Commonwealth Relations Office implemented policy. Paul investigates the protocols of the Ministry of Labour, including their administration of the *Westward Ho!* programme, which recruited 78,500 white migrant workers from the pool of post-war European refugees at a time when non-white colonial workers were discouraged from entering Britain. Spencer scrutinises the CRO records that deal with their largely successful attempts to persuade the Indian and Pakistani governments to disincentivise migration by increasing the costs of passports and introducing impedimentary bureaucratic procedures.

Like most revisionist accounts, Paul's analysis built on elements within the existing literature and this is most evident in her analysis of the British state's promotion of outward migration by white Britons to Commonwealth countries such as Australia, New Zealand and Canada and to the territories of European settlement in Africa. In introducing an edited volume published in 1990, Stephen Constantine noted that the enormous surge in emigration from the British Isles in the late 19th and early 20th centuries, which reached a peak figure in 1913 of 389,394 people, set a precedent for the inter-war period. Although these levels were never surpassed, Constantine records that during the 1920s 1,811,553 Britons emigrated. As late as the 1950s 652,000 Briton relocated to destinations outside Europe [131]. Strikingly, this extra-European emigration continued to be financed by the British state even as it was divesting itself of colonial authority. One of Constantine's contributors, Keith Williams suggests that in the 19th century emigration to the empire 'owed more to individual or family initiative than to state planning or directive.' This changed with the introduction of the Empire Settlement Act in 1922 which enabled the state to subsidise the passage of migrants to the dominions, assist with land settlement or even to provide agricultural training for migrants with little farming experience. The costs to the Treasury were justified on the grounds that emigration would alleviate problems of unemployment in the metropolis but the larger ideological context was provided by the racial theories of social imperialists, such as the novelist Rider Haggard and the politician Leo Amery. They believed emigration would vent social pressures at home, foster development in the wide open spaces of empire and demonstrate the vigour of the British people. Assessing the underlying motives of the pro-emigration lobby, Williams states: 'it was essential for eugenic reasons that the imperial "race" of "Greater Britain" should be a healthy, competitive and dynamic breed' [156: 26]. Two other contributors to Constantine's volume, Kent

Fedorowich and Michael Roe, published significant monographs which expanded on their original essays and dealt respectively with the efforts of the metropolitan government to encourage emigration to the dominions by British ex-servicemen and the tough bargaining strategies employed by dominion governments to attract white immigrants during the inter-war period [135; 148].

Potential migrants to the old imperial periphery continued to be offered financial assistance until 1972 but the later period has been less intensively studied than the pre-1939 era. Constantine suggests that this ongoing fidelity to the emigration project was sustained in its later phases by the persistent lobbying of Commonwealth governments who were able to mobilise sympathetic politicians in the metropolis [132]. Of those historians who do deal with the post-1945 era, most have been more concerned with the motives of the migrants than with the enablements of the executive and legislative framework. These historians, like their peers working on British immigration, have drawn on oral history, letters and diaries to capture the experiences and character of emigrants. The most closely scrutinised group have been the so-called 'Ten Pound Poms' who relocated to Australia and were the subject of a major study by A. James Hammerton and Alistair Thomson published in 2005. In common with Phillips and Phillips, the authors drew on evidence collected for a television programme, also called *Ten Pound Poms*, as well as oral histories and autobiographical accounts collected by researchers at the University of Sussex and La Trobe University. Most of their subjects had been beneficiaries of the UK-Australia Free and Assisted Passage Agreement of 1947 which enabled adults to travel to Australia for the sum of £10 at a time when the total costs of the long voyage were approximately £120. On occasions the accumulation of testimony tends to blunt some of the analytical purpose of the book, but Hammerton and Thomson offer some illuminating commentary. After examining a sample of 89 interviews, they found that dissatisfaction with British working conditions was the most frequently cited motive for emigration. The depressing effects of the British climate were the second most common reason and the authors note a surge in emigration following the Perth Commonwealth Games in 1962, which were broadcast to Britain in the midst of a particularly dismal winter. More generally the authors rely on qualitative rather than quantitative evidence and *Ten Pound Poms* gives a sense of the emotive and poetic quality of recording the experiences of ordinary people [138].

Questions of identity are integral to discussions of voluntary migration and Hammerton has recently suggested that a 'light cosmopolitanism', defined in terms of a more globalised outlook and associated with lifestyle choices rather than ideological commitment, was an important determinant for the last generation of emigrants [139]. By contrast Constantine is sceptical about the notion of a distinct British diaspora and cautious about the possibilities of finding a consistent pattern in the epistolary and oral testimony of the migrants [133]. The mere fact that historians are concerned with the choices made by British emigrants attests to the voluntary character of adult migration from Britain in the 20th century. This distinguishes their histories from those of migrants who were compelled to leave their homes, such as the British citizens who fled Uganda. The prevalence of coerced migration in the history of British decolonisation becomes still more evident from a study of people on the move in the old imperial periphery.

Migration around the periphery

Any account of the role of migration in the history of empire which focuses exclusively on relocation to and from the metropolis risks replicating the provincialism and historical myopia which have marked contemporary British debates about immigration. Arguments about the entry of workers and refugees are often as fraught in the successor states of empire as in Britain, as controversies regarding the free movement of people around the territories of the Anglophone Caribbean and New Delhi's disobliging attitude to the diasporic Indian community have demonstrated over the years. Two contrasting examples of population displacement on the verge of independence suggest that those transformative moments at which new nation states emerge have particular significance for historiographical debates about migration. The partition of India in 1947 and the detachment of the Chagos Islands from Mauritius in 1965 demonstrate a marked contrast in scale; the former involved the spontaneous movement of millions of people and the latter the carefully controlled movement of hundreds. What they have in common is ongoing geopolitical significance and contemporary resonance. Post-partition hostility between India and Pakistan has been the decisive fact in subcontinental politics since independence and was founded on arguments about frontiers and population displacement. The transfer of the indigenous people of the Chagos islands enabled Washington to establish military facilities on the pristine, newly depopulated island of Diego Garcia and these have proven integral to the projection of American military power in Asia, including the prosecution of wars in Iraq and Afghanistan. As well as exploring the political and strategic ramifications of these episodes, historians have shown a particular sensitivity to their tragic human aspect.

Yasmin Khan has described the process which accompanied the political division of South Asia as 'nothing short of a continental disaster' [23: 8]. What most parties intended to be a peaceful transfer of power turned into a human catastrophe which the governments of both the British imperial state and the successor governments of India and Pakistan were powerless to stop. Most commentators estimate that around 15 million people, which approximates to the entire present-day population of the Netherlands, left their homes. The violence which both caused and accompanied the great migration resulted in the deaths of between 500,000 and a million people, roughly equivalent to the number of fatalities experienced by the British army during the whole of the First World War. Although it is even more difficult to make assessments of the number of women abducted during the chaos, it seems plausible that as many as 100,000 became separated from their families and it is known that many of them were raped by their abductors. The key sites of migration were the Punjab in the west, where flight took place more rapidly and the violence was more intense, and Bengal in the east, where the fighting started earlier and continued for longer. In both locations people were on the move before the declaration of independence but it is not merely the fact that Britain retained ultimate juridicial control for much of the period which marks this as a key episode in imperial history.

From a historiographical point of view, the causes of the partition remain contested. In her influential account, Anita Inder Singh suggested that the divisive policies pursued by British colonial administrators during the Second World War created the circumstances in which they were eventually obliged to accede to the demands of Muhammad Ali Jinnah and the Muslim League for a separate state of Pakistan. On her account, British diplomatic manoeuvring, which was designed to contain Congress opposition to the war effort, 'incidentally encouraged Jinnah's league to anticipate that, when power had to be transferred after the end of the war, Pakistan would be in sight, whereas hitherto the prospect had been visionary'. Singh interprets the Cripps Offer of 1942, which included provisions for provincial secession, as decisive in facilitating partition [29]. In a more recent examination of the circumstances which attended the drawing of the frontier between India and Pakistan in the Punjab, Lucy Chester concludes that the extent of imperial influence over the partition settlement has been underestimated in the secondary literature. Her reappraisal of Cyril Radcliffe's role in the establishment of the new frontier indicates that British policymakers 'made good use of the atmosphere of pressure and fatigue in which all the leaders operated to move events in the direction most favourable to British interests' [21: xx].

Although Chester's work is revisionist in drawing attention to the dynamic influence of British imperialism in its dying days, it is traditional in the sense that it draws primarily on the written record generated by British and Indian elites. By contrast, a new history of Indian partition, rooted in the testimony of those who experienced it, has flourished in the last 15 years. The landmark book, which has been constantly cited in later publications, was Urvashi Butalia's *The Other Side of Silence*. Taking its apt title from a passage in George Eliot's epic novel of pre-Victorian provincial life, *Middlemarch*, the silence to which Butalia alludes is a consequence of established historical practices which muffled the voices of marginalised people. Butalia disavows any claim to be a conventional historian and there is evidence of this in the book's repetitions and acute self-consciousness. The numerous reservations which she enters about the truthfulness of her own account suggest a willingness to embrace subjectivity and mark the influence of poststructuralism and postcolonialism on her work. Butalia justifies her own frequent appearances in the text by endorsing Barthes' contention that the exclusion of the author from her own text merely generates the 'illusion of objectivity'. It is feminism which acts as a cynosure in guiding her away from the renditions offered by elites and towards those who have been neglected in conventional partition narratives: 'The search for a history of women then was

what led me to a search for the history of others' [126]. Her quest
begins with an intimate exploration of her own family history and
the circumstances which led to the estrangement of her uncle,
who stayed in what became Pakistan and converted to Islam, while
the rest of the family fled across the new frontier to India. Having
established that grand political narratives tend to disregard the
ramifications of partition in the intimate space of the family,
Butalia explores the suffering endured by women during the mass
migrations across the newly established frontier in Punjab. She
uses oral history testimonies from those willing to speak, memoir
literature and some governmental documentation to explore the
abduction, rape and murder of women either in their own locality
or during long treks across the border. Her evidence challenges
numerous orthodoxies, most notably the belief that violence was
always conducted by strangers from other communities.

The Other Side of Silence also raises questions about the significance of gender in the politics of partition. Butalia demonstrates
that many women were killed pre-emptively by their own families in
an attempt to uphold masculine notions of honour. Furthermore,
India's Abducted Persons Recovery and Restoration Act, which
became law in 1949, obliged women who had been separated during the partition to return to their families regardless of the circumstances of their abduction. The nature of their life prior to
their disappearance and subsequent events, which might tie them
to their new place of residence, were of less weight than the requirement to restore Indian national pride by recovering the women.
The most invidious consequence of the act was that women whose
children had been born in Pakistan after their abduction were
expected to leave them behind. On Butalia's account, underpinning the legislation was a gendered understanding of India as a
mother-country to which the fate of real mothers was subordinate.
In order to restore both the integrity of the Indian nation and
the masculinity of Indian men, abductees were obligated to abandon infants who were the outcome of their 'illegitimate' union
in Pakistan. As Butalia puts it: 'Only then would moral order be
restored and the nation made whole again, and only then ... would
the emasculated, weakened *manhood* of the Hindu male be vindicated' [126: 150]. This kind of cultural analysis of political events
is one of the more contentious aspects of the application of postcolonial theory; not only does it appear reductive by leaving political,

social and economic factors out of account but the claims themselves are often indeterminate, in the sense that it is difficult to
conceive what kind of evidence might either corroborate or refute
them.

More persuasive are Butalia's arguments that the marginalisation of women's experiences in accounts of partition are integral to
a wider politics of exclusion. Whereas much of the earlier historiography had focused on men and religion, Butalia's ambit extends
from the experience of women to other marginalised groups,
including the dalit, or, as Gandhi described them, Harijan, class.
In considering how minority groups were defined, and who was
responsible for these definitions, she questions the Hindu presumption that dalits fell on 'their' side of the confessional division.
Despite the productive nature of these enquiries a final caveat
must be entered concerning the originality of *The Other Side of
Silence*. Butalia tends to understate the extent to which the violence
of partition had featured in previous narratives. After emphasising
the novelty of her methods throughout much of the book, in the
concluding discussion of memory she notes that in the early phases
of her research she 'learnt not to feel complacent about being the
"first" – many, many others had been there before me' [126: 277].
Butalia does not name these others and readers are left to discover
the precedents for themselves; the most notable include, on the
nature of partition violence, G. D. Khosla's careful cataloguing of
local conflicts in *Stern Reckoning*; from an oral history approach,
Alok Bhalla's three volume anthology of stories about partition,
which are a mixture of factual experience and fictional invention;
and, from a feminist perspective, Nighat Said Khan's analysis of
the violence directed against women who fled to Pakistan, which
originated in the same project and shares the same themes as *The
Other Side of Silence*, but which was published first [122; 142; 143].

Despite the existence of these antecedents, a much richer
historiography on partition emerged after the publication of *The
Other Side of Silence*. Talbot and Singh have provided a full summary
of this literature but four brief examples give a sense of its breadth
[32]. After exploring their experience of migration, Gyanendra
Pandey concluded that there may have been as many as 250,000
dalit refugees in East Punjab by May 1948. He demonstrates that
they continued to suffer discrimination when the question of
land resettlement arose and were even subject to restrictions on

their freedom of movement inside independent India [144]. Joya Chatterji shifted the historiographical focus eastwards and suggests that the handling of the refugee crisis by the Indian government in West Bengal was 'a failure of catastrophic proportion'. Using anthropological data compiled by UNESCO, she catalogues the new state's inability to provide adequate relief and its counterproductive efforts to disperse those refugees who had established their own self-governing settlements. Considering the predilection of many governments for dispersal of refugee communities, her study has great contemporary relevance [130]. Ian Talbot has engaged in comparative urban history by focusing on Lahore, whose Hindu and Sikh populations fled to India during the partition violence, and Amritsar, which lost almost the entirety of its large, historically-rooted Muslim community during the course of a few months in 1947. Basing his analysis on responses to a poll conducted by Gallup in 1999 and on interviews undertaken in the two cities between 2000 and 2005, he concludes that the partition riots were orchestrated and that the widespread impunity allowed to the perpetrators of communal violence demonstrates the complicity of the British colonial administration in the disorderly last days of empire [152]. The issue of British culpability is also aired by Catherine Coombs who has utilised many of the techniques previously applied to marginalised groups in order to investigate the self-understanding of members of the Indian Civil Service. On her account the memoirs written by this administrative class characterised the experience of partition as comprising a disconcerting loss of prestige, a traumatic exposure to what was perceived as uncontrollable violence and a disempowering sense that manpower shortages and administrative blundering had exposed imperial vulnerability at a moment of grave responsibility [134]. What is striking about this analysis is that, in privileging the emotions of colonial administrators rather than the decisions they made, it reverses common historiographical practice, which seeks explanations for events in the reasoning of metropolitan agents and in which ordinary people are deployed to give a sense of the experiential texture of the rise and fall of empires.

Whereas this recent literature on Indian partition has been concerned with recording people's memories of events, those who have investigated the displacement of the Ilois population of the Chagos Islands have devoted much of their time to recovering potentially incriminating documents. Although only hundreds, rather than the millions of Indian partition, were relocated, the ongoing legal and diplomatic ramifications of the event have placed a premium on new evidence. In 1965 the British government incorporated the Chagos, with some other small islands previously administered as part of the Seychelles, into the British Indian Ocean Territory (BIOT) in order to facilitate the establishment of an American base which would provide a regional haven for the projection of Western military power in southern Asia in the midst of the Cold War. Although some of the BIOT islands were returned to the Seychelles at independence in 1976, the largest of the Chagos group, Diego Garcia, is still a British overseas territory. After officials ejected the island's residents it was repopulated with American service personnel and the nature of their activities remains a subject of speculation. Despite the best efforts of Washington and London to repel journalistic interest the claims of the Chagos refugees for compensation from the British government have made Diego Garcia a notorious episode in the history of decolonisation. Two developments have abetted this process: firstly, the Mauritian government has challenged Britain's claim to sovereignty over the islands in the Permanent Court of Arbitration in Istanbul and secondly, the former Libyan dissident and later minister, Abd al-Hakim Belhaj, has asserted that his American captors flew him to Diego Garcia while transporting him from Malaysia to Tripoli in 2004. The use of the military facilities on the island for the rendition of suspects is of particular significance following revelations that it was considered as the location for an American penal colony in which prisoners of war from Afghanistan were to be incarcerated. Fortunately for the British government, Guantanamo Bay in Cuba was chosen instead.

Given the vulnerability of the British government to compensation claims and to Mauritian irredentism, it is unsurprising that when a new tranche of documents pertaining to the origins of the BIOT were released in 2012 they were not particularly revelatory. When one of my dissertation students investigated the new material she found that the most striking theme to emerge was the British preoccupation with the presentation of their case at the United Nations. Officials were particularly concerned that the legal resemblance between the cases of the Chagos Islands and the Falkland Islands might offer Argentina an opportunity to press its claims to the latter. As early as 1965, the Foreign Office informed the Governor of the Seychelles, that, in responding to the expected international protests at the incorporation of the islands into the BIOT, 'our counter-arguments will have to avoid giving ammunition to Argentina which is sure to perceive the analogy with the Falkland Islands'.[3] Much of the legal issue hung on the question of the definition of a non-self-governing territory but the political issues arising were more straightforward: the paramount status accorded to the wishes of the Falkland Islanders was not be extended to the inhabitants of the BIOT.

It is this history of official dissimulation and international controversy which provides the context for the secondary literature on Diego Garcia. Peter Sand devotes the bulk of his short book to transcriptions of American and British documents from the 1960s and 1970s which reveal the determination of Washington and London to portray the permanent residents of the island as temporary contract labourers. Much of the material is illustrative of official attitudes to the population transfer. One Foreign Office mandarin stated at the time: 'Unfortunately along with the birds go some few Tarzans or Man Fridays whose origins are obscure, and who are hopefully being wished on to Mauritius etc' [149: 17]. In return for access to the depopulated island, the American government secretly offset the costs which Britain incurred in developing a nuclear missile system for Polaris submarines. As an expert in international environmental law, Sand is keen to catalogue the ecological damage caused by the construction of American military facilities in a location where development had been limited to the establishment of a small plantation economy [149]. By contrast, David Vine is an anthropologist preoccupied with how the exercise of American power overseas has affected the human rights of indigenous people. The title of his book *Island of Shame* reveals his perspective on the treatment of the Ilois. He uses many of the same documents as Sand but supplements them with descriptions of the impoverishment of the exiled families following their relocation to Port Louis in Mauritius. In a similar manner to Butalia, Vine acknowledges his partiality and gives a full account of the circumstances in which he became embroiled in the story. He supports the islanders' claim to compensation and pays careful attention to the case of the Bancoult family. The loss of their way of life is interpreted as a consequence of different forms of imperialism: 'taking the whole of the history of the Chagossians as a people, the islanders' struggle represents a challenge not just to US imperial power but more than five centuries of injustice tied to the global expansion of European empires' [154: 195].

Conclusions

The dramatic demographic transformations which occurred in the final years of the British Empire can be studied in a different way from earlier periods of imperial history because many of the participants are still alive to speak of them. For the Phillips brothers, with regard to Afro-Caribbean migration to Britain, and for Butalia, with regard to Hindu migration to India, this offered an opportunity to think about the experiences of their own families and then to reconsider the way in which the history of their communities has been characterised by outsiders [126; 146]. By contrast, expellees from Uganda living in Britain and from Diego Garcia living in Mauritius, have been the subject of studies by academics from outside their community, including Robertson and Herbert, and Vine and Sand [141; 147; 149; 154]. These were migrants who were coerced by the state because of the exigencies of decolonisation: in the first instance as a result of the targeting of those sectors of society which had, or were believed to have, collaborated or benefitted from British imperialism, in the second, as a consequence of the British government's Cold War alliance with the United States. The search for new documentation about Diego Garcia brings the study of migration back to questions concerning the exercise of political power and the strategic and economic interests which underpin imperial policy-making.

Most notoriously in the age of expanding European empires, the forced transportation of West Africans to the depopulated Caribbean had been underpinned by mercantile interests. Less well known is the later encouragement given to the outward migration of white Britons to the Americas, Africa, Asia and Australasia during an era of imperial dissolution. It is these events to which historians such as Belich and Constantine have drawn attention [121; 131]. The broader challenge which emerges for historians of migration is how to balance the experiential against the explanatory. Recording the memories of the migrants is important if the silences regarding subjects such as the partition of India are to be broken and if the history of women and the poor are to be included in the literature. In cases of voluntary migration such a project may also offer an understanding of motives. But the historic role which governments have played in either directing and facilitating, or preventing and impeding, the movement of people suggests that larger structures of political and economic power which underpinned decolonisation need to be considered. In the case of the ethnic Chinese in Malaya and the Kikuyu in Kenya, hundreds of thousands of people became subject to population controls, including forced relocation to sites of imperial superintendence, during the course of insurrection against British rule. Such resettlement was only one aspect of British counterinsurgency strategy, a subject that has generated some seminal historiographical controversies of its own.

4 Counterinsurgency, Intelligence and Propaganda

Military history is the scholarly field in which the concerns of the present day press most keenly on the study of the past, and no issue in British imperial history has greater contemporary relevance than that of the means by which agents of the colonial state suppressed dissidence and elicited complaisance in the last years of their rule. At stake are the personal fortunes of the survivors of colonial insurgency, the reputation and liabilities of the British state and a set of wider questions about how states conduct irregular wars against non-state actors. And for all of these reasons, historians interested in the role of the armed forces and intelligence services in policing the empire and fighting colonial counterinsurgency have often found themselves in conflict with the post-imperial British state over issues of access to the documentary record. Under the Waldegrave Initiative on Open Government, from 1993 the British government has attempted, on the one hand, to grant historians access to some previously classified material, while on the other, retaining its right to arbitrate on which historical documents are made available. Initially much of the intelligence material released under the initiative related to the pre-1945 era but over the last decade many more records from the Cold War period have been declassified and some of these have very significant implications for the history of decolonisation.

Executive control over this carefully calibrated strategy of openness has recently been challenged by the judiciary. The intervention of the courts was a direct consequence of the emergence of a revisionist literature about the Mau Mau insurgency in Kenya which has been particularly associated with two books published in 2005: *Imperial Reckoning* by Caroline Elkins and *Histories of the Hanged* by David Anderson [157; 166]. Although arguments continue about aspects of their work, even the most sceptical reviewers acknowledged that Elkins and Anderson had uncovered new evidence demonstrating that the British authorities had engaged in a concerted effort to cover up the brutality of the measures taken against the Kikuyu. Their work dented orthodox views regarding a distinctive British tradition of counterinsurgency based on the application of limited force. During the course of a legal case brought by former Kikuyu detainees the British government acknowledged the existence of a depository at Hanslope Park in Buckinghamshire where sensitive documentary material was stored. In October 2013, it was revealed that 1.2 million files dating back to 1856 were held at Hanslope Park, although not all of them relate to the history of the empire. At this stage it is impossible to predict what effect the uncovering of this archive of sensitive material will have on the historiography but it clearly signifies a further loosening of state control over the imperial archive. Whatever new facts do emerge they will not speak for themselves and the controversies over the past two decades about the use of military force, propaganda and intelligence during the last years of empire will provide a point of departure for any new schools of interpretation.

Colonial counterinsurgency

Debates about whether the British armed forces have a tradition which prioritises the employment of minimum force provide the context for recent developments in the historiography on counterinsurgency in the era of decolonisation. Definitions of what constitutes minimum force are contested but the term implies some effort to discriminate between actual and potential insurgents and the prioritisation of measures to win the 'hearts and minds' of the latter. As a corollary, it is usually interpreted as requiring a disavowal of certain kinds of extreme measures, such as torture and exemplary punishment. In the early 1990s somewhat acrimonious exchanges between Thomas Mockaitis and John Newsinger sketched out the nature of the arguments for and against the proposition that minimum force characterised British strategy. Mockaitis produced two volumes about British counterinsurgency, the first in 1990, dealing with the 1920s to the 1960s and the second in 1995, on what he described as counterinsurgency in the post-imperial era [176; 177]. Newsinger objected to

Mockaitis's contention that it 'would be difficult to exaggerate the importance of minimum force to British counter-insurgency' [174: 213]. Taking as a counter-example, the British suppression of Mau Mau, Newsinger suggested two conclusions: 'first of all that the Kenyan campaign was characterised by widespread beatings, torture, mutilations and shootings and second that this demonstrates that the doctrine of minimum force was not in practice adhered to' [181: 56].

In 2002 Newsinger published his own more critical analysis of Britain's late imperial wars which emphasised the widespread victimisation of civilian populations by the armed forces [180]. In response, Mockaitis has continued to defend the applicability of minimum force doctrines. In a recent restatement of the case he makes the unsupported and implausible suggestion that revisionists like Newsinger have been influenced by political correctness imported from the United States. Mockaitis's more substantive point is that minimum force doctrines were subject to interpretation and that their evolution over time points to their continuing influence as one factor among many in the conduct of British counterinsurgency. Furthermore, because the colonial security services were diverse in their composition, it is very often difficult to identify those occasions on which the British army was implicated in brutality. On Mockaitis's account this is particularly true of the Mau Mau war, which he identifies as exceptional because of the intensity of the violence employed [175]. My own scepticism about Mockaitis's arguments derives from evidence I uncovered during my research suggesting that civilians were targeted in other instances of colonial counterinsurgency. The Political Directive which governed the conduct of British forces during Operation Park in the Aden Protectorates demonstrates that the punitive approach to counterinsurgency was still operational in the Middle East in 1965. Non-combatants were offered only provisional protection in those instances where villagers agreed to evacuate their homes; in cases where they did not the directive stated: 'Casualties to women and children will have to be accepted.'[1]

But it has been the Mau Mau campaign which has had the greatest significance in the debate about minimum force. The two key revisionist figures are Caroline Elkins and David Anderson. Although, as Mockaitis's reservations indicate, their portrayal of British colonial brutality in *Imperial Reckoning* and *Histories of the*

Hanged remains controversial, they can be credited with tackling one of the great problems of imperial historiography, which is the imbalance between the vast written archive representing the views of various forms of imperial authority and the exiguous resources which historians can use to interpret the experience of imperial subjects [157; 166]. Both scholars employ material from the Kenyan National Archives in Nairobi. Anderson gleans key insights about the experience of those charged with capital offences from the court records of the Kenyan Ministry of Legal Affairs, while Elkins attends to the record of the Prisons Department. Some of the controversy surrounding Elkins's work concerns the use of interviews which she conducted with the assistance of a Kikuyu woman, Terry Wairimu, but this oral history material is supplemented with other kinds of evidence, including incriminating official documents, the desperate letters of detainees and the testimony of various British men and women who worked in Kenya including a rehabilitation officer, Eileen Fletcher, a Commissioner of Police, Colonel Arthur Young and members of the Church Missionary Society. What emerges from this new material is disquieting. During the process of interrogation or screening and the ensuing months or years of incarceration, Kikuyu men and women were humiliated, beaten and starved in labour camps. Some of the testimony offered to Elkins recorded horrific instances of sexual violation including the torture of women by the insertion of foreign objects into their vaginas and the castration of men. Elkins estimates that a large proportion of the Kikuyu population was sucked into the 'pipe-line' of labour camps, with those labelled as 'black' or committed Mau Mau being dragged ever more deeply into the system, while less committed 'grey' or 'white' detainees were subjected to crude indoctrination as a substitute for rehabilitation [166].

Whereas Elkins examines the experience of those who were interned without ever being placed on trial, Anderson concentrates on those who were charged with offences and in particular the 1,090 Kenyans who were hanged following guilty verdicts. At the centre of his analysis is an account of the greatest atrocity committed by the Mau Mau, the Lari massacre of approximately 120 men, women and children, killed in their homes because of their association with the loyalist Home Guard. As Anderson notes, many more innocent Kenyans were murdered in Home Guard reprisals than had died at Lari. From the official British perspective criminal convictions and public executions were necessary in order to deflect attention from the reprisals, reassure loyalist Kikuyu and white settlers, intimidate potential Mau Mau adherents and demonstrate that the judicial system could deal effectively with the criminality of the rebels. Anderson establishes that in pursuing the perpetrators of Lari, the judicial system was thoroughly corrupted: the list of capital crimes was extended to incriminate those that had consorted with individuals who threatened public order; confessions and witness statements were beaten out of suspects and the mere presence of an accused person at Lari was accepted as sufficient evidence of their participation in the massacres. Seventy-one of those found guilty were executed and all of those released or acquitted were immediately subjected to detention orders and placed in the 'pipeline' of labour camps. Anderson estimates that when the system of incarceration reached its peak in December 1954, 71,346 people were being detained and argues that there were significant parallels with the operation of the Soviet gulag [157]. It was historical analogies such as these which reviewers found to be one of the least digestible elements of the work of Anderson and Elkins but there was a general acceptance that the new work constituted a significant historiographical advance [164; 179].

Although both Elkins and Anderson made use of the gulag analogy, the former did so in the main title of the British edition of her book and this was occasionally taken as an opportunity to contrast her purported sensationalism with Anderson's more measured critique. The noisiest of Elkins's critics was not a professional historian but a television executive called David Elstein who had been responsible for the launch of Channel Five. Elstein took up the cause of Terence Gavaghan, a former Kenyan district officer who Elkins held culpable for the maltreatment of detainees. After Ofcom partially upheld a complaint brought by Gavaghan against an edition of the BBC *Correspondent* programme which had aired Elkins's allegations, Elstein took the opportunity to condemn the BBC for the unaccountability of its journalism. He extended his criticisms to Bernard Porter and Neal Ascherson who had given broadly positive reviews to *Imperial Reckoning*. The key issues arising from Elstein's critique concerned Elkins's estimate of the number of casualties in the conflict and the veracity of the testimony she collected from former detainees. While demographic analysis has dented her claims in the former regard, on the latter she has been vindicated by the British courts. On the penultimate page of *Imperial Reckoning*, Elkins attended to the Kenyan census figures for 1948 and 1962 which indicated that the growth in the Kikuyu population was much slower than that of other groups. She suggested that this could be explained by two factors: a larger number of deaths during the insurgency and a decrease in female fertility as a consequence of the traumas of war. She estimated the shortfall at between 130,000 and 300,000 and asserted that official figures of 13,000 Kikuyu casualties were a dramatic underestimate [166: 366]. Subsequent analysis by John Blacker indicated that Elkins was correct in identifying a demographic anomaly but that her upward revision was on too large a scale and failed to take account of tribal reclassifications between 1948 and 1962. While emphasising the number of imponderables on which all such estimates rest, Blacker utilises 'indirect techniques' of demographic analysis to extrapolate from more detailed census data available for 1969. After issuing a series of warnings about the provisional character of his calculations, he concludes that the number of excess deaths between 1949 and 1959 was between 30,000 and 60,000 and that a significant portion of these may be accounted for by an increase in infant mortality as a consequence of the malnourishment of mothers and the policy of enforced villagisation of the Kikuyu. In questioning Elkins's quantitative methods, Blacker produces a sobering analysis that reconfirms the damage the Mau Mau war caused to Kikuyu society [162].

In terms of her qualitative methods, Elkins's efforts to circumvent the self-justifications offered in the official record by employing oral history techniques have demonstrated the extent to which that record has been sanitised in an attempt to hide British culpability. She advised five former Kikuyu detainees who in June 2009 filed a legal claim against the British government for the torture and mistreatment they had endured during the insurgency. In her account of the legal arguments which followed, Elkins suggests that the formal determinism of judicial procedure offered a haven from academic sniping. In the court, the role of the historian was narrowed to the laborious but clearly defined task of supplying documentary evidence which could be evaluated by the judiciary before a definite outcome was obtained [6]. Lawyers for the British government attempted to prevent a trial by arguing, first, that the government in London did not have legal responsibility for the actions of the Kenyan government during the 1950s, and then, that the claims had been brought too late and breached the statute of limitations. These arguments were rejected by Mr Justice McCombe in rulings issued in July 2011 and October 2012.

Three further key developments occurred between 2009 and 2012: one of the original five claimants, Susan Ngondi, died and another, Ndiku Mutua, withdrew; Elkins was joined as an historical expert by Anderson and Huw Bennett; and in April 2011, the British government was obliged to acknowledge, despite previous denials, that they held additional evidence about the Mau Mau war, comprising approximately 1,500 Kenyan files, at the secret Hanslope Park archive in Buckinghamshire. The cases of the three remaining litigants, Jane Muthoni Mara, Wambugu Wa Nyingi and Paulo Nzili, did not go to trial because on 6 June 2013, the British Foreign Secretary, William Hague, issued a statement of regret and offered £20 million in compensation to 5,228 Mau Mau veterans. Strikingly, the British government also agreed to fund the raising of a monument to the victims of the war. Lawyers have begun to investigate whether the case sets a precedent for other litigants to pursue grievances from the era of Britain's late empire, particularly in the case of Malaya, while historians have a daunting task in unpicking the revelations from the Hanslope Park disclosure. This latter undertaking became more formidable in October 2013 when it was revealed that the archive contained many more documents than had previously been estimated, with apparently six metres of material on Rhodesia alone, as well as further documentation about non-colonial affairs, including the defection of the Cambridge spies, Guy Burgess and Donald Maclean. Anderson has already utilised some of the initial Hanslope Park releases to explore the extent to which senior officials authorised the so-called dilution techniques which were designed to force submissions from the most committed Mau Mau detainees. Official comment on the murder of a man called Kabugi at Mwea camp in October 1958 reveals that the Kenyan Governor and Attorney General condoned the use of extreme violence. When it was discovered that 11 detainees had been beaten to death at Hola camp in March 1959, senior officials followed the precedent set in the Kabugi case and blamed the overly zealous actions of prison guards. Anderson suggests that historians will need to look again at the way in which the colonial state established the norms and institutions which permitted such abuses [158].

Outside of the courtroom and the recesses of the Manor House at Hanslope Park, the Kenyan insurrection of the 1950s continues to elicit academic scrutiny, with Huw Bennett and Daniel Branch offering significant new perspectives. Bennett reintegrates the new historiography on Mau Mau into the ongoing debate about the application of minimum force doctrines, while Branch turns back to another tradition of interpreting the conflict as a civil war among the Kikuyu. In his detailed exploration of interactions between the regular army and the civilian population, Bennett offers a nuanced endorsement of revisionism. He argues that 'restraints imposed by international law and minimum force had little place in the army's counterinsurgency in Kenya' [160: 657]. This tendency was most marked in the period between October 1952 and June 1953 when the regular army was implicated in beatings, extra-judicial murders and mass evictions as part of a strategy to enforce complaisance on the Kikuyu [159]. This analysis prompted a lively exchange with Rod Thornton who argued that Bennett had failed to distinguish sufficiently clearly between the different elements of the security forces in Kenya [160; 182]. In his most recent work, Bennett has maintained that the British army implemented punitive policies against the Chinese population in the first years of the Malayan insurgency. He interprets this partly as an outcome of intelligence failures, which made it impossible to distinguish friend from foe, but suggests that it also reflected cultural assumptions about the racial inferiority of colonial subjects [161].

Branch's approach is radically different from Bennett's. In the conclusion of his monograph *Defeating Mau Mau*, he demands that historians reconsider the role of anti- and non-nationalists in decolonisation. Although divisions among the Kikuyu over Mau Mau have long been recognised and even accentuated in some of the historiography, Branch's work is helpful in demonstrating the priority which the post-independence governments of Kenya have given to shaping perceptions of the war. The governing Kenya African National Union (KANU), under the leadership of Jomo Kenyatta and Daniel Arap Moi, portrayed the Mau Mau insurgency as a straightforward conflict between European colonialism and African resistance. This camouflaged the fact that former African colonial loyalists who had fought against the Mau Mau were flourishing under KANU's new dispensation. Only with KANU's electoral defeat in 2002 did it become expedient for a new government to pursue the politics of colonial redress as part of a critique of the entrenched conservatism of local elites. Even in these circumstances, Branch records that his investigation of loyalism unsettled many of his Kenyan interviewees. Despite this wariness and the slipperiness of loyalism as a concept, Branch concludes that those who collaborated with the British were motivated by local circumstances, including revulsion against the tactics of Mau Mau, rather than by the often clumsy 'hearts and minds' propaganda of the British [163].

Branch's work is part of an emergent post-revisionist trend which extends beyond the Kenyan case, as the work of Matthew Hughes on Palestine and Karl Hack on Malaya demonstrates. The former describes arguments about the use of coercion as 'sterile' and adds a note of polemic by suggesting that critics of counterinsurgency tactics are 'often on the political Left and uninterested in the details of military service'. However, he also asserts that the emerging 'ethnography of nastiness is a valuable empirical exercise, hampered by the morally bankrupt policy that shredded and destroyed archival material' [172: 585]. In his analysis of the Arab Revolt in inter-war Palestine, Hughes concedes that the heavy-handedness of British practices, including the destruction of property as a measure of collective punishment by the army and the torture of detainees by police and prison guards, served 'to weaken, perhaps to shatter, Palestinian rural village society, creating in the process lawlessness, hunger and social dislocation'. He also provides new details on atrocities committed by British forces including the use of a land mine to kill Arab captives at al-Bassa in September 1938 and the caging of starving detainees at Halhul in May 1939. In his conclusion, however, he returns to the familiar comparative frame of reference and preference for abstraction which are the enduring elements of orthodoxy. British tactics are characterised by Hughes as 'relatively speaking, humane and restrained the awfulness was less awful – when compared to the methods used by other colonial and neo-colonial powers operating in similar circumstances, an achievement, of sorts' [173: 354].

If Hughes's post-revisionism leans more towards older orthodoxies, Hack maintains a foot in the revisionist camp. The titles of some of his earlier essays on British counter-insurgency tactics in Malaya, such as 'Screwing Down the People', attest to his eagerness to challenge complacency about the application of limited force and the winning of hearts and minds [170]. Later articles have warned against the danger of over-compensating for the failures of the earlier historiography and even suggest that a 'herd mentality' has developed among rampaging revisionist historians in search of further incriminating evidence. Hack suggests 'the pendulum is over-correcting, from the period of the 1950s to the 1990s that exaggerated the degree of British wisdom and moderation, to a current phase of over-focusing on coercion and abuse as defining characteristics of campaigns and their phases' [171: 679]. Mention of a phased approach is crucial to Hack's analysis of British strategy in Malaya which, he argues, proceeded from an initial period of counter-terror between 1948 and 1949, to a more nuanced blend of controlled coercion and persuasion designed to instil confidence among the population, and finally, after 1952, to a period of inten-sified hearts and minds operations which was marked by more centralised control and better intelligence. On this account, the defining characteristic of British strategy during the Malayan emer-gency was neither coercion nor persuasion but one of spatial and population control, as manifest in the creation of the new villages which transformed the geography of the Malayan countryside [171].

The publication of four major monographs about Britain's experi-ence of post-war colonial counterinsurgency in the last five years has been helpful in distilling the findings of detailed campaign studies. Andrew Mumford is sympathetic to the revisionist trend and emphasises the ineffectiveness of British counterinsurgency tactics, while Benjamin Grob-Fitzgibbon acknowledges the coer-civeness of military methods but remains broadly sympathetic to British goals; Aaron Edwards reasserts traditional views regarding Britain's purportedly distinguished tradition of small-war fighting, and, other than a brief foray against Elkins, largely pretends that the controversies which date back to the Newsinger-Mockaitis exchanges 20 years earlier do not exist [165; 169; 178]. The most comprehensive analysis is provided by David French whose 2011 monograph, *The British Way in Counter-Insurgency*, is particularly notable for its comparative approach, which contrasts with the case study methodology of much of the literature. Rather than the usual chronological march through different campaigns, French examines the key elements of British counterinsurgency strategy using data taken from ten imperial territories. In material terms the context for these wars was the relative financial and military weakness of the colonial states of the periphery, while the ideological framework was provided by a tendency to equate opposition to colonial rule with criminality rather than political grievance. According to French both aspects impelled policymakers towards the use of coercion and this was enabled by legal innovations in the form of Orders in Council issued in the metropolis which equipped Governors with arbitrary powers. Distinctive features of these campaigns included the employment of exemplary force against civilians, ranging from curfews and fines to the establishment of free fire zones, the forced resettlement of people accompanied by food denial in proscribed areas, and the mobilisation of the RAF to bomb and rocket regions of upcountry insurgency [167].

In dealing with insurrectionists or suspected insurrectionists, French believes that the British were guilty both of destroying property and mistreating detainees and attempting to cover up the facts when scandals emerged, but that they did not engage in extra-judicial killings. Although British rhetoric focused on conciliation, development and winning hearts and minds these were of marginal significance. There is little or no evidence that progress was made in refining tactics over time. Outcomes, whether failure in Palestine or success in Malaya, were usually the consequence of factors largely outside direct British control [167]. In summarising the historiography French contends that the orthodox focus on hearts and minds operations has been employed to support 'a Whiggish view of decolonisation that portrayed the way in which the British left their empire as having been an orderly and dignified process of planned withdrawal'. Such an interpretation, French argues, is mistaken: 'The foundations of British counter-insurgency doctrine and practice were coercion not kindness. They sought to intimidate the population into supporting the government rather than the insurgents' [168: 758].

Intelligence and propaganda

The preoccupation of much recent historiography with unvarnished methods of coercion in colonial counterinsurgency may appear incongruent with the great interest historians have shown in studying intelligence and propaganda as a means of exercising what is sometimes described as soft power. Any element of paradox can be resolved by noting two other features of the historiography: firstly, as a glance at the contents of the journal *Intelligence and National Security* will demonstrate, the Cold War rather than the colonies has been of greatest interest to intelligence historians; and secondly, when they have studied intelligence and propaganda in a colonial context it has generally been in its role as an auxiliary to counterinsurgency, as is evident from two monographs by Rory Cormac and Calder Walton [189; 210]. Although studies of post-war British information policy generally have a Cold War focus, Greg Kennedy and Christopher Tuck recently collected together a series of essays analysing the role of propaganda in late imperial conflict. On the basis of this scholarship they endorsed French's challenge to the assumptions that the British pursued a policy of moderation in response to insurgency in the empire. They suggested: 'Britain has not been blessed with a uniquely effective understanding of influence activities nor has it been especially successful.' On their account the inadequacies of propaganda strategy provide the relevant context for the post-2001 problems encountered by the British armed forces in Iraq and Afghanistan [199: 10].

Before examining more of this work on intelligence and propaganda, it is worth attending to the most controversial issue in the field which concerns the measures taken by the state to restrict access to sensitive intelligence material. In one sense the situation in this regard has greatly improved, to the extent that it has been possible for Christopher Andrew, Keith Jeffery and Richard Aldrich to write well-informed histories of the Security Service (MI5), which acquired responsibility for the colonies in 1931, the Secret Intelligence Service (SIS/MI6), which under the Attlee Doctrine of 1948 was prevented from operating in the Commonwealth and the colonies, and the Government Communications Headquarters (GCHQ), which ran its own overseas empire of signals intelligence during the years of decolonisation [183; 185; 197]. As the subtitles of their books indicate, Andrew's history was authorised whereas Aldrich's was not and they differ over the extent to which governmental records can provide an effective picture of intelligence operations. Aldrich's suspicion that an official 'history policeman' controls access to the most sensitive documentation has been corroborated by the Hanslope Park discoveries. His scepticism does not derive solely from the superintending of official documentary releases but also from the historical practices of departmental records officers who favoured the preservation of policy documents rather than organisational records [184].

Aside from the Hanslope Park revelations, evidence is also accumulating that the destruction of records was more systematic than previously thought: Edward Hampshire has analysed the determined policy of burning the Malayan records and Caroline Elkins suggests similar policies were implemented in Kenya [7; 166: xii]. I was once informed that many Aden records ended up at the bottom of the Indian Ocean as the fleet departed in 1967, although some clearly survived for deposit in the India Office Library where they can be easily accessed by researchers. Despite the widespread evidence of the suppression of sensitive material, Andrew and Walton have asserted that criticisms of official caution over the release of documents can be 'largely refuted by examining declassified British intelligence records.' On their account it is the indolence of colonial historians, who have yet to incorporate these records into their accounts, rather than official censorship, which is to blame for deficiencies in the historiography. According to Andrew and Walton many of the documents which have been released do not show the intelligence services in a positive way and attempts to excise material can be readily identified because of the use of sequential serial numbers [211]. Excluded from this general indictment is the work of Philip Murphy, whose article on the role of intelligence in the Central African Federation demonstrated that the attitude of the SIS on colonial issues was politicised, as manifest in their sympathy for the white settlers. On the question of the relationship between record-keepers and historians, Murphy is in the same camp as Aldrich. The first sentence of his article reads: 'The role of intelligence agencies in the process of British decolonization has not so much been ignored by historians as systematically concealed from them as a matter of government policy' [203: 101].

A yet more radical critique of the role of government in suppressing historical evidence is evident in the work of Mark Curtis and Stephen Dorril, whose methods are informed by the traditions of radical journalism. Their approach is evident from the way they deal with events on the imperial frontier in two extremely sensitive, parallel cases from the first half of the 1960s, in both of which British intelligence agencies were implicated in undermining foreign governments. During this period, the British authorities were accusing President Sukarno of Indonesia of subverting the newly established post-colonial state of Malaysia and President as-Sallal of Yemen of sponsoring insurrection in the British colony of Aden. There is a historiographical consensus that British counter-measures went well beyond public denunciations and entailed the sponsorship of raids across the frontier into Indonesia and Yemen, the dissemination of black propaganda designed to desta-bilise the Sukarno and as-Sallal regimes and the making of clandes-tine contacts with groups opposed to the Indonesian and Yemeni governments. However, Curtis and Dorril offer interpretations of these events that are more critical than those of many conven-tional historians. In the case of Yemen, Dorril's central concern is to reveal the extent to which the British government sponsored the independent Anglo-French mercenary organisation which assisted the Royalist forces in their opposition to as-Sallal's Republican gov-ernment. His arguments are generally persuasive but his sources are frustratingly difficult to pin down. There is no doubt that the mercenary force in Yemen did acquire assistance from some shady, external sources and that both current and retired British civil and military personnel were implicated, including the founder of the SAS, David Stirling, and a member of the colonial administration in Aden, Anthony Boyle. As Dorril points out, some of these shenanigans were exposed by the Egyptian newspaper *al-Ahram* and the British *Sunday Times* in 1964. Reservations about his account concern the extent to which mercenary activity was spon-sored by British intelligence and, in particular whether the Foreign Secretary, Alec Douglas-Home, really did express enthusiasm for 'an unofficial operation' at a meeting with Stirling in March 1963 and then, when he became Prime Minister, authorise 'full support for the royalists' [192: 684–689]. On neither issue do Dorril's notes provide the necessary corroboration for his analysis of Douglas-Home's actions.

Academic historians such as Simon Smith, Clive Jones and Rory Cormac offer a clearer sense of the documentary foundations of these arguments. Smith, for example, quotes the recollections of the British minister, Nigel Fisher, that Harold Macmillan author-ised 'very substantial help to the Royalists' and these are freely avail-able at Rhodes House Library (201); but he interprets such covert operations in the wider context of London's determination to act independently of disapproving officials in Washington [31]. Jones reaches almost the opposite conclusion to Dorril and suggests that the British government was 'decidedly lukewarm' about mercenary activity. On his account mercenary operations in Yemen should be analysed as an example of the kind of covert operations which 'remain beyond the power of the state to either sanction, control or indeed curtail' [198: 718]. Similarly, Cormac characterises British intervention in the Yemen civil war as cautious and defensive and argues that the records of those metropolitan institutions responsible for covert action, including the Joint Action Committee, demonstrate that they wanted to restrain the 'gung ho' advocates of more extreme policies [189]. My own attempts to piece together the details of the clandestine RANCOUR operations from official documents led me to conclude that Dorril was correct to argue that the British were much more heavily implicated in subverting the Republican regime in Yemen than was admitted at the time, but that their preferred choice of proxies were not the mercenaries but the dissident tribes across the Yemen frontier. Furthermore, subversion of this kind long predated the 1962 Yemeni revolution and needs to be placed in that context [200].

There are similarities between the RANCOUR programme and the clandestine campaign against the Indonesian government in Borneo which was codenamed CLARET, not least in the evidence they provide of the willingness of British policymakers to infringe on territorial sovereignty and deploy black propaganda in order to destabilise foreign governments. The key difference is that, while the Republican government in Yemen survived the civil war despite British-sponsored subversion, President Sukarno's Indonesian regime collapsed in 1966 and a bloodbath ensued. Curtis goes as far as to accuse the British government of 'Complicity in a Million Deaths', which is the title of the chapter in *Web of Deceit* he devotes to the astonishingly brutal purge ostensibly directed against the Indonesian Communist Party (PKI) but which encompassed the murder of hundreds of thousands of people believed to have some form of association with the Indonesian left. Sukarno was targeted by Western intelligence both because of the tactical alliances he had established with the PKI and because his government was sponsoring incursions into those territories in northern Borneo which had been incorporated into Malaysia. Based on material released under the thirty-year rule that he collected for an

Observer article in 1996, Curtis asserts that 'British and US planners supported the slaughter to promote interests deemed more important than people's lives' [190: 397]. In his view, Western culpability rests on five counts: they initially encouraged the army to act against the PKI in order to undermine Sukarno, they suspended their operations along the Indonesian frontier in Borneo to facilitate the anti-leftist purge, they disseminated propaganda designed to generate hostility to Sukarno and the PKI, they supplied a 'hit list' of dissidents to the army and they provided arms to those who perpetrated the killing.

The evidence which Curtis presents relating to the 'hit list' and arms supplies implicates Washington rather than London but some of the other accusations have been corroborated by historians of Britain's confrontation with Indonesia. In his careful analysis, David Easter suggests that the West probably did not instigate the failed coup of 1965 which precipitated the massacres but indicates that in its aftermath the British, American, Australian and Malaysian agents fomented anti-communist feeling in Indonesia through the dissemination of propaganda. He quotes the Foreign Office's self-assessment that they had been 'blackening the PKI's reputation within Indonesia and outside' and suggests that this insidious information policy gave impetus to the mass slaughter of civilians undertaken by the army [194]. Easter also demonstrates that British signals intelligence and propaganda work played a central role in the clandestine CLARET cross-border raids into Indonesian territory which were first authorised in April 1964 while Sukarno was still firmly in control of the country [195]. Christopher Tuck, who has examined the CLARET operations in most detail, argues that they were intended as an interim and largely defensive measure. Despite their apparent success, they were inspired by British military pessimism about the prospect of maintaining the post-imperial dispensation in Malaysia. Operational discontent with the refusal to authorise an escalation of action against Indonesia peaked during the period of the massacres when political considerations apparently held sway [208; 209]. Though less sensationalist in tone than *Web of Deceit*, the work of Easter and Tuck partially confirms Curtis's assertion that British policymakers were eager not to distract the attention of the Indonesian army back to the frontier once they had begun their assault on the PKI and that black propaganda emanating from the West facilitated the violence.

The Indonesian and Yemeni cases illustrate the priority which British intelligence accorded to the defence of the colonial frontier but for a wider view it is necessary to turn to more synthetic work by Walton and Cormac. Both have used recently declassified primary material to reconstruct the colonial intelligence environment as independence approached. Although, Walton in particular emphasises the potentially transformative impact of the Hanslope Park material, his book *Empire of Secrets* is, as he acknowledges, a preliminary reassessment which was published as some documents were being transferred into the public domain. Many of the episodes Walton discusses are therefore already familiar to students of intelligence if not to a broader general audience. Much of his new analysis pertains to the methods the British government employed to cover the traces of its intelligence involvement in the colonies, particularly in the case of Malaya, where the destruction of records has left a particularly large hole in the archival record. In analytical terms Walton argues for the primacy of the Cold War and the Soviet threat in determining the conduct of British colonial intelligence, but this too may be regarded as a provisional judgement, given that London sometimes found itself attempting to persuade Washington that not every colonial nationalist should be regarded as a communist. The most striking and original aspect of Walton's work is the evidence that he uncovers concerning the continuation of British intelligence activities in the old imperial periphery after independence. This phenomenon again attests to the dynamism and adaptability of late imperialism and the indeterminate nature of political independence. For example, both Kwame Nkrumah in Ghana and Jawaharlal Nehru in India were surprisingly receptive to British requests to retain their colonial intelligence apparatus [210].

Cormac's research agenda is narrower but more sharply focused than that of Walton. Borrowing from the work of political scientists, such as Robert Jervis and Graham Allison, and taking advantage of Joint Intelligence Committee (JIC) files which have accumulated since the 1990s, Cormac undertakes an examination of colonial intelligence in counterinsurgency campaigns. His key findings are that bureaucratic politics, organisational processes and cognitive distortions had a significant impact on the effectiveness of these operations. Bureaucratic politics, or turf wars as Cormac describes them, were evident in the attempts of the Colonial Office to resist the JIC's infringements into their domain and in their criticisms of the crude imposition of a Cold War agenda on all colonial conflicts. Cormac also suggests that organisational inefficiencies hampered efforts to improve the performance of British colonial intelligence in the late 1940s and early 1950s. The integration of the JIC into the Cabinet Office from 1957 enabled it to play a more effective role in influencing policy during the Cyprus and Aden insurgencies than it had during the Malayan war, when it remained essentially a servant of the British Chiefs of Staff within the Ministry of Defence. One particularly significant cognitive impairment was 'mirror imaging', which was evident in the assumptions that other states behaved in the same way as the British state and even that insurgent groups were state-like in their behaviour [188].

At present, the balance of the new historiography on intelligence and the end of empire is tilted towards those territories in which an insurgency occurred and this is reflected in Walton's preoccupation with Palestine and Malaya and Cormac's four case studies of Malaya, Cyprus, Aden and Oman. Hakeem Tijani's work on Nigeria and my own on the Caribbean offer the beginning of a new analysis of the way Cold War considerations encouraged local governors to adopt illiberal peacetime policies in the years immediately preceding independence. We put our case for a new focus on these activities in similar ways: I suggest reversing the historiographical vector which seeks to trace the impact of colonial events on the superpower conflict, and to examine instead the way in which the Cold War influenced decolonisation; and Tijani declares that his objective is 'to remove British anti-communist policies from the footnote of decolonization as it embarked on tactics and strategies towards combating the communists' expansionism in Nigeria' [207: 49]. In the Caribbean, it was the activities of the Jamaican Ferdinand Smith, who had spent 30 years as a labour organiser in the United States, which preoccupied the security services, while in Nigeria it was another Marxist trade unionist, Nduka Eze, who was identified as a threat to the smooth ordering of decolonisation. In the late 1940s and early 1950s British governments extended the new Cold War fighting apparatus of the metropolitan state into the colonies and as radical, well-educated Marxists with connections to the international communist movement, Smith, Eze and their followers became targets of the intelligence agencies. Perhaps more significant than the monitoring of their activities were the wider measures undertaken to hinder the spread of communist ideas in the Caribbean and West Africa, including restrictions on freedom of movement and the suppression of communist literature. Passports and travel documents were denied to those planning to travel to eastern Europe and suspected communists were prevented from entering Nigeria and the Caribbean islands. Bans on communist literature also played a significant role in both instances. These restrictive policies were taken up with enthusiasm and deployed for their own purposes by local anti-communist politicians including Tafawa Balewa in Nigeria and Norman Manley in Jamaica [201; 207].

Of still more interest to British intelligence than Smith and Eze were Cheddi and Janet Jagan of British Guiana whose story has many contemporary resonances. Cheddi Jagan was the leader of the People's Progressive Party which won the pre-independence Guianese elections of 1953, 1957 and 1961, while Janet Jagan was an American citizen and Communist Party member who met Cheddi while he was studying dentistry in the United States. Over the last decade historians have taken a great interest in the intelligence aspects of Guianese decolonisation and in particular the role that American intelligence played in averting the possibility of the Jagans establishing 'another Cuba' on the South American mainland. Stephen Rabe, and Robert Waters and Gordon Daniels have detailed the manner in which the CIA, in collaboration with American trade unions, aggravated racial tensions between Indian-Guianese supporters of Cheddi Jagan and African-Guianese supporters of his rival, Forbes Burnham. In 1963, at a time when Guiana was still a British colony, the Burnham faction organised what Waters describes as the world's longest general strike in an effort to cause sufficient chaos to prevent Jagan from leading the country to independence. Strikers were sustained by subventions from the CIA under a covert operation codenamed 'Flypast' [204; 212]. American-sponsored subversion brought an unprecedented degree of communal violence to British Guiana but, as I argued in *Ordering Independence*, Washington's ambition to replace Jagan with Burnham only succeeded because the British Colonial Secretary, Duncan Sandys, introduced a new electoral system based on the Israeli model of proportional representation and funded rival Indian-Guianese parties prior to the 1964 elections [25]. Burnham secured a victory at the polls and led Guiana to independence, but his premiership was scarred by corruption. He also recanted on his status as an American protégé by establishing close ties with the Soviet bloc during the 1970s. Placing these events in the context of the Afghan and Iraq interventions of the 2000s, Richard Drayton suggests that Western chicanery in installing Burnham punctures the 'myths of Anglo-American virtue' on which the case in favour of liberal interventionism rests and highlights the dangers of 'blowback' from covert action [193].

Yet there is a great deal more to tell about this story. For instance, in 2011, 39 plump Security Service files about the Jagans were released covering the period up to 1961, while those for the later and even more controversial years remain classified. This may make Cheddi Jagan the most closely monitored of all anti-colonial politicians and an initial reading confirms that he was in regular contact with the Communist Party of Great Britain and with Soviet-backed international organisations, including the World Federation of Democratic Youth and the World Federation of Trade Unions. What they also reveal is the astonishing capacity of the British state for surveillance during the Cold War and it is difficult not to interpret the findings in the context of contemporary debates about the surveillance material supplied to *The Guardian* and the *New York Times* by Edward Snowden. During his numerous visits to Britain Cheddi Jagan's conversations were recorded by devices installed in various locales including hotels, his letters and those of others were opened and copied, his telephone conversations were monitored and he was followed for almost every minute of most days by Special Branch personnel. Additionally, MI5 recruited a number of unidentified informers who reported on Jagan's activities. Perhaps the most significant documents are those which record British politicians talking about the Jagans, rather than to them, because they indicate that the intelligence services were independently monitoring the communications of MPs associated with the Movement for Colonial Freedom, including Fenner Brockway, Ian Mikardo and Barbara Castle. For example, details of an inconsequential conversation between Brockway and an MCF official about Janet Jagan's gratitude for the warm reception her husband had received in London were culled from an outgoing MCF line on 11 June 1957.[2] Walton's investigation of the surveillance of the Kenyan nationalist Peter Koinange, who was regarded in British official circles as a dangerous renegade, similarly uncovered evidence that the communications of the Congress of Peoples Against Imperialism were monitored and that the intelligence services were keeping files on Brockway and Castle [210: 263].

One element of British strategy for containing the Jagans was to blacken their reputation in Guiana but in her pioneering work Susan Carruthers suggested that previous conceptions of late imperial propaganda were too narrow and that imperial propagandists were as much concerned with metropolitan and international audiences as with colonial ones. Persuading British citizens and global opinion formers of the legitimacy of British aims and methods was, on Carruthers' account, one of the key components of British counterinsurgency doctrine. She provides some particularly suggestive examples of the dilemmas of colonial propagandists in Palestine, Malaya, Kenya and Cyprus. In the case of Cyprus, which is relatively neglected in the study of colonial counterinsurgency, the Cold War context was problematic because, although the leader of the Cypriot insurgents, George Grivas, found the politics of Hitler more congenial than those of Lenin, it was expedient for the British government to give voters the impression that the island had become a Mediterranean haven for leftists. They were assisted in doing so by right-wing British newspapers such as the *Daily Express* which disseminated the tendentious official reading that Cypriot insurgents were inspired by communism. In a particularly agile publicity manoeuvre, the *Express* annexed colonial warfare to partisan domestic politics by implicating the Electrical Trades Union in terrorism on the grounds that the union had offered £20 to assist with the legal defence of Cypriot leftists who had been caught up in indiscriminate British security sweeps on the island. In illustrating some of the perplexities generated by this kind of propaganda strategy, Carruthers examines the case of the murder of a British soldier's wife, Margaret Cutliffe, during a shopping trip in Famagusta. News of her death elicited indignation from the press which was inconvenient at a moment when the Macmillan government was seeking to negotiate a resolution to the war. The accusations of appeasement which inevitably followed drew on domestic British resentments that had initially been fostered by the government [187].

On the international front, Carruthers suggests that the American audience was regarded as particularly important.

A *Daily Telegraph* journalist, Douglas Williams, was despatched to Washington at the initiative of the Governor, John Harding, with the task of improving the image of Cyprus's colonial government. Cultivating international and domestic opinion in this way was usually accorded greater priority than repairing the tattered information machinery located in the colony. But the largest theme tackled by Carruthers is one which has greatest ongoing currency, namely the relationship between propaganda and terrorism. In the context of a greatly expanded international news media, there was a warranted tendency in the 1940s and 1950s to believe that insurgents employed violence tactically in order to generate publicity for liberationist causes. One question which vexed colonial officials was what to call their adversaries, and perhaps the most important criterion in finding an answer was to employ the appellation most likely to delegitimise them. 'Bandit', which was initially applied to the Malayan insurgents, had the requisite criminal connotations but had the disadvantage of obscuring the Cold War overtones of the war at a time when it was important to alert American audiences to Britain's role in containing Soviet and Chinese influence. In May 1952, therefore, 'bandits' became 'communist terrorists' in the official lexicon of British counterinsurgency [187].

A significant danger arising from the compelling work of scholars such as Walton, Cormac and Carruthers is that the literature about intelligence and propaganda in a colonial context may be swallowed whole by the historiography of post-1945 counterinsurgency and the Cold War. One countervailing trend, evident in the work of Kate Utting and Sanjoy Bhattacharya, has focused on the Second World War as a turning point in the development of British colonial propaganda. During that conflict the power to coerce subject peoples into complaisance was circumscribed by the pressing need to maintain armed forces at the fighting fronts and the requirement to persuade African and Asian audiences of imperial legitimacy became correspondingly more urgent. Total war necessitated the mobilisation of colonial resources and it was particularly important to retain the allegiance of civilian populations that were close to the front line, such as those in Bengal and the other states of Eastern India which are examined by Bhattacharya. He suggests that British apprehensions about the twin dangers of anti-colonialism and Japanese invasion led to a renewed emphasis on propaganda as a means of influencing those workers who were essential to the war effort. Another theme of his work concerns the bureaucratic obstacles which made it difficult to implement a centralised and coordinated information policy at a time when many district officials were showing sympathy for the Indian National Congress and its campaign of non-cooperation. It is this emphasis on the constraints which hindered British efforts to disseminate their message, and an awareness of the multifaceted nature of propaganda in an imperial context, which causes Bhattacharya to reject the notion of an imperial hegemony in which complaisance was induced by offering imperial subjects a diet of misleading information [186].

Similar themes to those discussed by Bhattacharya are evident in the work of Utting although she is more ambitious in seeking to trace the propaganda trail from the Ministry of Information and the Colonial Office in London to the work of individual information officers in East Africa. Her argument that the period between 1939 and 1948 marked a transformation in the nature of British propaganda is supported by evidence of the Colonial Office's determination to advertise the merits of more egalitarian forms of partnership; this, she suggests, was an alternative to older and more established notions of trusteeship, in which the priorities of the imperial state inevitably took precedence over the interests of the imperial periphery. Under this new wartime dispensation information officers such as Harry Franklin in Northern Rhodesia were able both to gauge the state of local opinion and take measures designed to bolster the morale of civilians and soldiers. She identifies 1943 as the moment when 'imperial propaganda found a successful dual combination of inspirational leadership and a new mission' [202: 103].

Although the flow of new material about colonial intelligence and propaganda has enabled historians to gain a better understanding of the nature of intelligence and propaganda in a colonial context, historians still need to ask broader questions about the purpose of all this activity and this requires some attention to be paid to the impact of theory; in this regard, the work of historians, most notably Priya Satia and Martin Thomas, on the formative stages of modern intelligence gathering is likely to prove of lasting value. Both focus on the Middle East as an imperial theatre in which modern intelligence gathering techniques were elaborated and both draw on the postcolonial notion that culture played a key role in shaping structures of power. Thomas is more wide-ranging in the sense that he is concerned with intelligence gathering in both urban and rural contexts; he examines human, signals and image intelligence and investigates commonalities and differences between French and British imperialism across much of the Middle East and North Africa. On the basis of this analysis he offers a clear statement of the purpose of intelligence gathering in an imperial context: 'the colonial state amassed information about subject populations to guarantee its monopoly over the use of force and to impose its authority on a subject population designated to play arduous but subordinate parts in a European dominated economic system' [206: 18]. When it failed to achieve these purposes it was often because of the distorting effect of cultural preconceptions of the kind that Edward Said labelled Orientalist. For example, the British authorities were surprised by the nationalist uprising in Egypt after the First World War because of the belief, which was sustained rather than challenged by the focus of intelligence reports on Egyptian elites, that the mass of the population was incapable of uniting around a shared idea. The limits of the intelligence order were revealed again in Palestine in 1936 when, as in Egypt in 1919, the intelligence services failed to predict the outbreak of an Arab revolt. Thomas demonstrates that counter-intelligence operations were central to British strategy for containing and then subduing these colonial rebellions. He concludes that the colonial state should be seen as an intelligence state and that the employment of the intelligence apparatus was an expedient means of avoiding resort to totalitarian methods of policing [206].

There are two significant differences between Thomas's *Empires of Intelligence* and Satia's *Spies in Arabia*. Firstly, although Satia gives a nod to Marx's materialist conception of history, she places the distorting effects of Oriental prejudice at the centre of her analysis, while Thomas asserts that intelligence gathering proceeded with a clear purpose which was to shore up an economic order that prioritised Western interests. In some respects this difference reflects tensions in Said's work, which sometimes proceeds on the basis that occidental understanding of the Orient was entirely defined in terms of cultural subjectivities while at other times suggesting that ideas of eastern inferiority served specific material purposes, namely the conquest and domination of the Middle East by Britain and France. Secondly, although they share similar views about the exploitative character of colonial intelligence and the significance of its cultural underpinnings, Thomas argues that the work of the colonial security state was often mundane or to put it at its bluntest 'more office work and record keeping than cloak and dagger.' By contrast, Satia has a more elevated view of the British intelligence order in the Middle East which she asserts was intimately connected to currents in modern literature and philosophy. Her investigation of social and family networks is striking in its demonstration of these networks. For example General Allenby's key intelligence adviser, Richard Meinertzhagen, was the nephew of Beatrice Webb and his diaries were partly inspired by encouragement from the positivist philosopher Herbert Spencer, and the daughter of the novelist Aldous Huxley. Another intelligence agent and politician, Aubrey Herbert, had established friendships with many famous authors including John Buchan, Rupert Brooke and Hilaire Belloc [205].

What emerged from these influences was a romantic culture of intelligence, which proceeded by intuition and feel, rather than close observation and logic; it could also generate peculiar and brutal results, most obviously in the way in which it validated the policy of aerial policing which began in Iraq and spread to other Middle Eastern territories in the inter-war period. On Satia's account British agents who had immersed themselves in the culture of the Middle East 'perceived a basic congruence between the liberty of action of the aircraft and the desert warrior, both operating in empty, unmapped, magical spaces.' This correspondence was embodied in the figure of T.E. Lawrence who after his wartime exploits in Arabia joined the Royal Air Force. His views on the commonalities of the two experiences are quoted by Satia: 'What the Arabs did yesterday the Air Force may do to-morrow. And in the same way – yet more swiftly' [205: 242]. A further consequence of this non-rational intelligence culture was the pervasiveness of conspiratorial thinking. During the 1920s there was widespread recognition that a new, clandestine form of empire was emerging and, in the absence of reliable information, increasingly bizarre conspiracy theories flourished in both Britain and the Middle East. These ranged from the comprehensive theories of the agent, Norman Bray, who claimed that 'Asiatic intriguers' in Morocco, Algiers, Tunisia, Egypt, Western Arabia, India and Constantinople were run from a command centre in Switzerland, to more general fears in Britain that the government was surreptitiously importing Oriental and autocratic practices from Arabia into domestic political life [205].

Conclusions

It would be presumptuous to prescribe the research agenda in the field of late colonial counterinsurgency in any great detail but some of the issues which are likely to elicit the interest of future historians can be anticipated. The first tasks will be to assimilate whatever new evidence emerges from the ongoing declassification of Security Service files and the uncovering of Hanslope Park material, as well as to assess the significance of the losses and redactions. Revisionist studies of colonial counterinsurgency have already offered an effective challenge to an orthodoxy based on a heavily edited colonial archive that had been cleansed of the most incriminating material [157; 166; 170; 180]. Despite the judicial victory secured by Elkins, historiographical controversies never end in unalloyed triumph, and a new post-revisionist trend is already evident in the work of Hack and Branch [163; 171]. This may well signify a shift in focus towards a more careful consideration of the uses of what might be termed 'soft power' rather than 'hard' coercive and punitive methods.

Recent work on propaganda and intelligence can also be interpreted as part of this emergent literature. Although 'gap filling' is sometimes disparaged as a lazy route into the historiography, the balancing out of geographical and thematic coverage is also of importance. Recent articles by Panagiotis Dimitrakis and Chikara Hashimoto on the post-1945 intelligence apparatus which sustained Britain's informal empire in Cyprus and the Middle East are genuinely helpful in extending historiographical horizons [191; 196]. The accumulation of additional evidence also requires the fashioning of new theoretical tools, which is where the work of Thomas and Satia assumes particular significance [205; 206]. Whether thinking, as the former does, in terms of broader material structures, or in the latter's case, of the philosophical zeitgeist, they both attach the history of inter-war intelligence to wider historical currents. The subject on which military and intelligence historians are often most reticent is the question of whether war-fighting or spying serve a larger purpose; as we shall see in the next chapter, and as might already be evident from the discussion of attempts to contain the influence of Smith, Eze and Jagan, such activities were often intimately connected to the dramatic changes taking place in the relationship between labour and capital in the last years of the British Empire.

5 Capital and Labour

Decolonisation is often depicted as a process of political reform in which power was transferred from representatives of European imperialism to a new class of nationalist politicians. In such accounts conflicts tend to take place at the conference table and are about incremental shifts in the balance of constitutional authority. The Indian Round Table conferences of the 1930s and the Lancaster House conference on Kenya of the early 1960s are pivotal moments in this kind of narrative. But there is a different tradition of writing about 20th century imperialism which is concerned with the relationship between European capital and African, Asian and American labour. Whereas the termination of European political control was marked by the celebrations which accompanied independence, there was often continuity in the sphere of economics. Although strikes and industrial relations reforms may be identified as key events in securing liberation, the old imperial periphery remained dependent on Western capital long after the new national flags were hoisted above government buildings. Relations between business and workers before political independence did not change dramatically in its aftermath and this observation may even destabilise the very notion of decolonisation. Theories of neo-colonialism suggest that economic production in the old imperial periphery continues to generate conflict between Western capital and non-Western labour and that the balance of advantage still lies with the former. One of the difficulties which arises in examining this process is that scholars tend to specialise either in the history of business or the history of labour and each has its distinct traditions.

In thinking about the role of capital within the British Empire in the 20th century the major and often competing themes are those of adaptation and decline. A variety of statistics tracing levels of production, share of world trade, outward and inward investment can be used to depict the state of the British economy; these can then be measured from different points in time and in relation to figures about other countries or the global economy generally, in order to estimate how far and how fast Britain was declining. When these statistics are placed alongside political transformations, what emerges is a more complex picture which looks more like adaptation than decline and this is one of the implications of the decisive intervention Peter Cain and Antony Hopkins made in the historiography over two decades ago. Their emphasis on the adaptive capabilities of Britain's gentlemanly capitalists is consonant with the view that 20th century British imperialism was still characterised by dynamism and innovation [216; 217]. Business historians were particularly responsive to the work of Cain and Hopkins, although many of them questioned their emphasis on metropolitan developments as the determining factor in the rise and decline of the empire. In the same vein an implicit critique is offered by those labour historians who have reconsidered the role of colonial workers in challenging the impositions of Western capitalists and the complacency of British imperial administrators. By emphasising the resistance to the overbearing economic and political direction of the European powers, first Frederick Cooper and later Martin Thomas switched the focus away from the City of London and towards people such as miners, agricultural labourers, factory workers and dockers, whose labour was essential to the successful operation of the British imperial system [241; 256].

Capital

When P. J. Cain and A.G. Hopkins published two complementary volumes of *British Imperialism* in 1993 they were self-consciously attempting to alter the terms in which the economics of British imperialism were debated and this ambition was encapsulated by the prominence they offered to the concept of gentlemanly capitalism. Their first book, subtitled *Innovation and Expansion*, dealt with the rise of gentlemanly capitalism and its role in imperial expansion during the period from 1688 to 1914, while the second, *Crisis and Deconstruction*, covered the years from 1914 to 1990 and examined the strategies of adaptation employed by gentlemanly capitalists during the era of decolonisation. Although the constitution of the gentlemanly capitalist elite changed over time, their power was sustained by deep historical roots in the landed aristocracy and by a symbiotic relationship with the imperial bureaucracy. As economic power inside British society shifted, the character of the gentlemanly capitalists altered and by the 19th century they were more likely to have accumulated wealth through investments in commercial activities such as banking, shipping or insurance than by the exploitation of land. Cain and Hopkins found plentiful evidence to demonstrate that gentlemanly capitalists were deeply embedded in British political life. Their support for British expansion overseas generated substantial overlap with the class of politicians and civil servants and predated the emergence of an industrial middle class. As a consequence, those whose wealth derived from land or finance or services established an early and sustained political advantage over those who wished to uphold the new priorities and interests of manufacturing [216; 217].

Some of Cain and Hopkins's analysis of imperial expansion and consolidation had been anticipated in their earlier articles and it was their discussion of the survival of the gentlemanly capitalist elites during the 20th century which was particularly novel in 1993 [219]. For this later period, they argued that the importance given to defending the value of sterling reaffirmed the prerogatives of the gentlemanly capitalist class. On Cain and Hopkins's account, the status of the pound was prioritised because the financiers of the City of London had more influence over government than the industrial bourgeoisie or other classes in British society. In the 20th century their predominance was still rooted in the shared values instilled in both city gents and imperial agents by the common biographical trajectory of public school and Oxbridge. Cain and Hopkins offer statistical evidence to support this interpretation but it is the career of a single individual, Ralph Furse, which best illustrates the institutional sway of the gentlemanly capitalists. Furse was from a 'well-connected gentry family'; he was educated at Eton and Oxford, related by marriage to the influential Montagu family and between 1919 and 1948 he was the official responsible for recruitment to the Colonial Office. As he travelled the empire, 'no matter where he went, Furse was certain to run into other men of influence who were known to him through family connections' [217: 25].

Having sketched the means by which the gentlemanly capitalists adapted and prospered against competition from the industrial class, Cain and Hopkins substantiate their thesis with examples drawn from the formal political empire in Africa and India and the informal commercial empire of the dominions, South America and China. Perhaps the most significant evidence of the imprint of gentlemanly capitalism on late imperial management can be found in the unexpectedly low priority accorded to the retention of the periphery as a market for British manufactured goods and the correspondingly high priority attached to the export of primary products or commodities from the periphery to the wider world. One instance of this phenomenon was the scuppering of plans to establish preferences for intra-imperial trade after the First World War. Although such a policy would have facilitated British exports to British colonies, it would have jeopardised British financial services which were dependent on an international system of open markets that extended beyond the empire. This liberal trading order disintegrated in the 1930s despite the best efforts of the gentlemanly capitalists to save it, but their influence was again evident at the Ottawa conference of 1932. The system of imperial preference inaugurated by the bilateral agreements made at Ottawa was designed to meet the danger posed to sterling by the collapse in international commerce. Taken as a whole the tariffs and regulations governing imperial trade after Ottawa gave a competitive advantage to India and the dominions at the expense of manufacturing in the British metropolis. This peculiar outcome can be explained by the fact that sterling was the means of exchange for trading inside the empire. By enhancing the fortunes of the emerging sterling bloc as a whole, rather than privileging metropolitan interests, the Ottawa system fortified the currency, even at the expense of British exporters [217].

According to Cain and Hopkins, retaining India as a market for British goods was less of a priority for gentlemanly capitalism than securing India's future as a user of sterling. India was a vital market for the textile exporting industries of north-west England and its loss in the inter-war period had catastrophic effects on employment in the region; but what mattered for Britain's imperial administrators was that the Government of India Act of 1935 enforced a policy of financial rectitude on the nationalists at the point when they were beginning to acquire greater political authority. This strategy was vindicated when India, which had become Britain's largest colonial creditor, remained in the sterling bloc at independence in 1947. By this stage, the system of imperial preference was being dismembered, a new liberal trading order was under construction and the pound was imperilled by the enormous demand for imports from outside the empire and Commonwealth. In this environment, the key economic function of the imperial periphery was to export commodities to the rest of the world, including rubber and tin from Malaya, oil from the Middle East and agricultural products from Africa. The surpluses which accumulated from this export trade were deposited in London where they increased the pool of hard currency reserves that was essential to keep the current account in a measure of equilibrium and thus sustain the value of the pound. Cain and Hopkins conclude 'it is no coincidence that the regions of greatest economic value in the period of reconstruction were also those where Britain's determination to perpetuate her control was particularly marked' [217: 280].

The ambition of the Cain and Hopkins thesis allowed plenty of scope for dispute on a variety of fronts. Two issues arising from debates about decolonisation which proved particularly significant were the nature of capitalist influence over late imperial policy-making and the extent to which the fortunes of the sterling bloc impeded independence in some colonies. Many of those who investigated the former question found not a unified class of British capitalists and colonial bureaucrats but a series of conflicts between them. In his analysis of post-war Egypt, Nigeria and Kenya, Robert Tignor offered numerous counter-examples to the portrayal of a harmonious and smoothly articulated relationship between agents of capital and state. In emphasising the significance of financial factors in decolonisation, Tignor's work is consonant with that of Cain and Hopkins but at the outset he declares that their 'rationalized and economist view must, of course, arouse suspicion. Its ability to explain developments in the three countries dealt with here proved to be limited' [232: 12–13]. On his account, decolonisation was as much about the expulsion of British finance as about the forced exit of imperial administrators and soldiers. In Egypt, British governmental inattentiveness to the concerns of business contributed to the eventual sequestration of foreign assets by Nasser's government in the late 1950s. While the British government prioritised political and strategic considerations, the influence of British companies such as Barclays, which was targeted because of its role in cotton exportation, was expunged. This renationalisation of the Egyptian economy, on Tignor's account, 'marked as sharp a break with the past as any of the more celebrated events of the first decade of Egyptian independence' [232: 137–138].

In Nigeria the British government established marketing boards in 1946 despite trenchant opposition from mercantile interests. According to Tignor the ostensible purposes of these institutions were to act as a buffer between local Nigerian producers and the volatile global market in commodities but in practice they outraged both British businessmen and local nationalists. The former were irritated by the colonial state's encroachment on their control of the export trade, while the latter were incensed that the enormous surpluses accumulated by the boards as a consequence of rising commodity prices were invested in British banks. In another example of the influence of presentism on historical writing, Tignor traces the corruption of Nigerian politics to the mishandling of the development board funds by the first generation of nationalist politicians. Only in Kenya did Tignor find evidence that the colonial state was solicitous in its dealings with British business but even in that instance, their efforts proved unavailing. Although British administrators went to great lengths to secure a virtual monopoly for the Lancashire-based firm, Calico Printers Association, over East African textiles, they lost control of production in 1954. Tignor is sceptical about the successful adaptation of British commerce during the era of decolonisation and notes that the Asian investors who supplanted European capitalists in Kenya had previously been treated with disdain by the colonial state [232].

As Tignor's findings demonstrate, much of the resistance to the Cain and Hopkins thesis is a product of uncertainty regarding the level of generalisation required to deal with a very large empire over a very long time. In her detailed study of the influence of British commercial firms during the last years of British rule in the Gold Coast, Sarah Stockwell questions the success of the gentlemanly capitalists in advancing commercial interests inside the metropolitan government. She is sensitive to the distinctiveness of the Gold Coast case which is evident from the unusually prominent role played by individual businessmen. Edward Spears of Ashanti Goldfields Corporation was the most significant example.

He became embroiled in local controversies to the extent of offering encouragement and publicity to local opponents of Kwame Nkrumah. These interventions were not licensed by the colonial government and Stockwell asserts there is no evidence of 'the cosy City-Whitehall nexus' portrayed by Cain and Hopkins [232: 232]. Like Tignor, Stockwell focuses on agency, or the actions of particular individuals such as Spears, in determining the course of events and even suggests that differences in personality influenced different outcomes [230]. Turning to Asia, Maria Misra criticises the notion that financial orthodoxy dictated policy towards Indian nationalism in her analysis of the role of business interests in the inter-war period [227; 228]. Similarly, the leading expert on the role of commercial factors in Malayan decolonisation, Nicholas White, has emphasised that 'on key Malayan issues business leaders and public servants were often at loggerheads' [233; 234; 187]. The gist of these critiques is their emphasis on variations between countries and business sectors. Cain and Hopkins, by contrast, were aiming for a broader understanding of British imperial history and focused on structures, including elite networks and patterns of investment, in order to offer generalised explanations for the changing character of British global influence. When asked to comment on these anomalies, Cain and Hopkins argued that some variation was inevitable: 'It is scarcely surprising to find that details of time and place do not replicate, perfectly, the broad principles governing a worldwide empire' [218: 215].

Despite his scepticism about the notion of a close alliance between British capitalists and administrators, White offered a helpful and nuanced analysis of reactions to the Cain and Hopkins thesis. While reiterating that government and business had distinct interests and that lobbying of the former by the latter usually proved ineffective, he acknowledged that Cain and Hopkins had identified a new form of 20th century British imperialism 'based not upon the empire's significance as a dumping ground for manufactures or as a source of cheap raw materials but on the importance of colonial primary production in bolstering sterling' [235: 563]. This observation shifts the focus back to the second important question which arises when the Cain and Hopkins thesis is applied to the era of decolonisation: what was the relationship between the maintenance of the sterling bloc and the gradual demission of power to newly independent governments in the colonial periphery? In separate studies Gerold Krozewski and Allister Hinds largely corroborated Cain and Hopkins's arguments that the management of sterling determined the political strategies pursued by the British government at the end of empire. Hinds identifies the disastrous experiment of 1947, when sterling's value shrank on becoming full convertible, as a turning point. Nationalist challenges in Malaya, Nigeria and the Gold Coast during the late 1940s had to be resisted because they were the key dollar-saving and dollar-earning territories of the empire. Events moved swiftly during the following decade and by the end of the 1950s it was estimated that the costs to the British Treasury of funding development in the colonies were likely to outrun any further potential benefits of colonial dollar-earning now that the pound was more secure. The restoration of a semblance of financial order to the sterling area alongside the political problems posed by the rise of colonial nationalism thus facilitated decolonisation [223].

A similar picture is presented by Krozewski but he is rather bolder and even combative in demanding a greater emphasis on patterns of British financial investment in discussions of decolonisation. He is particularly scathing about the inadequacy of political accounts of the end of empire that do not consider the role of international finance, without which 'it is impossible to understand the changes in imperial relations during the final phase of empire' [224: 5]. According to Krozewski, the move towards full sterling convertibility in 1958 strengthened the arguments for decolonisation because 'the treasury and the Bank of England would no longer have to step in to support colonial pooling arrangements or to underwrite colonial loans on the London market' [226: 67]. In his encounter with Cain and Hopkins he acknowledged the pertinence of the financial theme which runs through their analysis, while arguing that they failed to consider sufficiently the social and political discontinuities between the 19th and 20th century [225].

More recently a number of historians have examined the impact of Britain's empire of commodities. Steven Galpern offers a clear statement of his thesis at the outset of his book on oil and post-war imperialism: 'British officials viewed the Middle Eastern oil trade as critical not only to preserving sterling's international stature but also to protecting the currency from ruin, reinforcing the already powerful imperative to safeguard the nation's strategic and economic interests in the Middle East' [221: 2]. On his account, the tendency of British governments to look first to the defence of the currency was less an outcome of informal networks and more a consequence of the formidable influence which the Treasury exerted over the late imperial bureaucracy. When they turned their attention to the balance sheet of empire, officials could not fail to acknowledge Middle East oil as their most prized asset. Although Iran had never formed part of Britain's formal empire, the Anglo-Iranian Oil Company's refinery at Abadan constituted the largest investment of British capital overseas. Galpern notes that the AIOC exerted enormous influence in the province of Khuzistan where the refinery was located and Iran 'was perceived as a British colony of sorts' [221: 83]. In illustrating its significance, Galpern discusses the uncompromising reaction of the Treasury to the nationalisation of the refinery by the new Iranian Prime Minister, Muhammad Mossadegh in 1951. The leading Treasury official Leslie Rowan argued that reprisals against the Iranian government were imperative because a negotiated settlement 'would almost certainly nullify any measures which His Majesty's Government was proposing to take to re-establish the position of sterling' [221: 113]. In a notorious covert operation, the British and American government overthrew Mossadegh's government in 1953. During the subsequent reordering of Iran's oil affairs, the British insisted that the new consortium, which now included American companies, should trade in sterling and maintain exchange controls to prevent any inflow of dollars.

Galpern also describes the disastrous Suez war of 1956 as a 'sterling rescue operation gone wrong'. He argues that the decision to invade Egypt was at least partly determined by the fact that Nasser's nationalisation of the Suez Canal Company occurred at another period of vulnerability for the pound, which was moving towards a position of free convertibility. By the time sterling became fully convertible in 1958 lessons had been learned. In their negotiations with Kuwait prior to the country's full independence in 1961, the Treasury and Foreign Office adopted subtler methods in dealing with a state which was 'a major shareholder' in the sterling area [221: 202]. As a result Britain retained indirect control over Kuwait's enormous sterling surpluses and achieved some success in limiting Kuwaiti investments outside the sterling area. Galpern concludes by suggesting that current American policymakers should take heed of the British experience as they seek to manage the decline of the dollar.

While seeking to retain their grasp on Middle East oil, Sarah Stockwell has pointed out, British policymakers in the 1950s were also engaged in a state-led 'mineral rush' for access to Africa's resources. She emphasises the strategic rationale which underpinned the search for the uranium and thorium to sustain British nuclear ambitions [231]. Such endeavours were largely fruitless, but much greater success attended efforts to exploit the continent's prized copper resources. The operations of the mining industry of Northern Rhodesia have been examined by Larry Butler and Ian Phimister. In *Copper Empire*, Butler records that British bombers of the Second World War carried two miles of copper wiring, while a battleship would contain roughly two million pounds of copper. He investigates the three cornered conflict over the division of the copper spoils which was conducted between imperial administrators, overseas investors and the nationalist movement and their supporters in the metropolis. Official estimates indicated that during the 1930s Northern Rhodesia generated £2.4 million in revenue for the British exchequer and received only £136,000 of funding from the Colonial Development and Welfare Fund. Perhaps unsurprisingly, Butler concludes that the development of the Northern Rhodesian copper industry 'was an example of large-scale overseas investment which brought rapid benefits to the metropole' [215: 300].

Copper Empire also offers an insight into how the taxation of their profits antagonised overseas businessmen, including South African investors in Rhodesian Anglo-American (RAA) and the American corporate interests which eventually predominated in the Rhodesian Selection Trust (RST). Anti-colonial critics in Britain had a different perspective from these businessmen and noted that both taxation revenues generated for the British exchequer and royalties, remittances and dividends paid to private interests overseas, precluded the accumulation of capital in Northern Rhodesia. Butler discusses the role of Rita Hinden of the Fabian Colonial Bureau who condemned the enormous profits which accrued to private investors as a consequence of the royalties paid to the British South Africa Company (BSAC), for mining rights. BSAC had administered Northern Rhodesia until 1924 and maintained close ties with the RAA. Attacks on the company's historic privileges led to a first deal in 1949, in which BSAC guaranteed that the lucrative mining rights would revert to the state in 1986, and then to a second in 1964, by which the newly independent Zambian government acquired the rights immediately [215]. On the vexed historiographical question of the relationship between business and politics, Butler asserts the primacy of political interests, which contrasts with Phimister's emphasis on the role of financial imperatives in determining labour relations. Phimister notes that copper mining became ever more remunerative in the early 1950s and explores how issues of profitability, technological change, cost structures and the operation of the colour bar in employment shaped a new relationship between capital and labour. He also reasserts the significance of material factors in driving companies such as RST to replace better paid white mine workers with cheaper African labour. Apparently progressive corporate attitudes to race were, on Phimister's account, often an outcome of changing corporate interests defined in fairly narrow terms of cost and profitability [229].

After political independence, the Zambian economy was hampered by the inadequacy of the country's social and material infrastructure which had been designed by the British around the needs of the copper mining industry. Investment from the People's Republic of China has rectified some of these deficiencies and gradually improved Zambia's economic fortunes. These circumstances raise questions about economic development and in particular the very late and novel effort British imperial administrators made to address the deficiencies of private enterprise. An official five volume history of British colonial development was published in 1980 but, aside from this very narrowly conceived project and some detailed studies of particular development projects, most notably the African groundnuts scheme, this is another historiographical field where there is significant scope for further study. For example coverage of the Attlee government's role in instigating the Colombo Plan, which was intended as a Marshall Plan for the empire, was noticeably thin until Krozewski, Shigeru Akita and Shoichi Watanabe published their collected volume on the subject in 2015 [213]. These lapses of historiographical attention are particularly surprising given that development studies has become a significant academic field in its own right. Perhaps the best current starting point is still the 20-year-old work by Michael Havinden and David Meredith, which utilises statistical analysis to answer the question of why British colonial development failed.

Although they address many of the structural problems which made it difficult for British colonial administrators to modernise colonial economies, at the centre of Havinden and Meredith's thesis is the notion that proponents of colonial development in the late imperial era lacked the requisite understanding of overseas conditions to pursue effectively economic expansion in the territories they governed. In explaining the attitude of imperial administrators to industrialisation they state:

> The theory of economic development held by the colonial authorities thus remained at the rather superficial level of attempting to maximise production of primary products for export without any real investigation as to how export earnings could be used to achieve diversification and development in the economy as a whole. [222: 306]

Havinden and Meredith suggest that early schemes embodied in the 1929 Colonial Development Act had insufficient funding to have much impact: 'a nominal amount of £1 million a year spread over 45 underdeveloped countries and 55 million people disappeared almost without trace' [222: 167–168]. Even with an expanded remit and increased funding, the Colonial Development and Welfare (CDW) Act of 1940 remained an instrument for conserving social peace and a familiar economic order which centred on the cultivation of land. According to the statistics proffered by Havinden and Meredith for the wartime period, 28% of CDW funding went to agriculture, 22% to water supply and irrigation, 12% to communications and 12% to health and sanitation. It might be argued that post-war spending of CDW funds on education did provide a progressive variation to this theme, which Havinden and Meredith acknowledge only in perfunctory fashion. Despite this caveat, there is a marked contrast between the concern of British developmentalists to promote efficient production in traditional agricultural sectors, and the nationalist demand for economic diversification and accelerated industrialisation. These differences were reinforced during the 1940s when two agencies, the Colonial Development Corporation and the Overseas Food Corporation, sprang up at the behest of the metropolitan government with the specific aim of increasing commodity production and the supply of food from the colonies to the metropolis [222]. According to Havinden and Meredith the impulse to use public capital to fortify traditional agricultural practices in the tropical empire was closely connected to the desire to preserve existing social systems. This in turn raises the question of the kind of work which was available to the people of the periphery and to the ideological and institutional frameworks in which this work was conducted.

Labour

The failure of development policy was not just a consequence of the insufficiency and misdirection of capital resources but was tied to broader questions concerning resistance in the colonial periphery to the imposition of European models of labour conduct. In their efforts to administer a global empire, British colonial bureaucrats could claim a degree of proficiency in fiscal matters but they were perplexed by the issues of gender, class and race which arose as they attempted to reform industrial relations. The most influential chronicler of these misapprehensions has been Frederick Cooper. In *Decolonization and African Society* Cooper compared the efforts of France and Britain to control labour in their colonial territories and found that in both cases 'African workers forced colonial planners who wanted to think about development to think instead about the labour question' [241: 110]. For the British, thinking about development in Africa was a novel activity and in the interwar period they were disinclined to consider the possibility that the movement of Africans into cities would challenge the European conception of a stable, rural African society based on ancient tribal allegiances; but, as Cooper demonstrates, urbanisation did generate new class affiliations and from 1935 strikes by workers became a persistent feature of African politics and society.

On Cooper's account colonial administrators developed a binary way of thinking about these transformations based on the notion that casual, migrant workers who represented traditional African practices, could be replaced by regular settled workers who would pioneer a potential European future for the continent. Actual African conditions were more complex than this and when workers refused to conform to imperial expectations the resulting conflicts were ascribed to their culture. Cooper quotes the African Labour Efficiency Survey of 1949 which offered perhaps the bluntest expression of this way of thinking when it declared that the

African worker 'is ineffective in industrial techniques by the very nature of his birth, his upbringing and his native culture' [241: 240]. The politics of stabilisation adopted during the late imperial period were intended to replicate European forms of industrial organisation, including the establishment of trade unions which were conceived as a replacement for what the Labour Colonial Secretary, James Griffiths, described as 'the traditional African society of family or tribal mutual aid' [241: 329]. To the consternation of imperial policymakers, attempts to impose European industrial relations practices offered new opportunities for resistance to colonialism in Africa and strike action often proved effective in achieving material gains for workers. At the same time the race and gender assumptions which underpinned imperialism ensured that Europe could never really be replicated in Africa. Cooper demonstrates that on such basic and easily quantifiable measures of progress as income, imperial administrators never accepted that black Africans should obtain the same level of material reward as white Europeans. For example, in East Africa an elite of black Africans in the senior civil service were subject to an informal rule which stipulated that they receive three-fifths of the salary paid to Europeans in equivalent posts (445). While administrators were preoccupied with race, Cooper asserts that the 'gendering of African workers was so profound it was barely discussed. The entire discussion of danger and of promise – of the African worker becoming productive – assumed a male worker' [241: 266].

The gendered assumption that the industrial worker is masculine persists to the present day and has been challenged by Samita Sen who has charted the marginalisation of Indian women employed as wage labourers in sectors often thought of as male preserves. During the period between 1890 and 1970, Sen notes, there was a decline in the number of women involved in the production of jute and coal, and colonial legislation in 1928 formally banned women from working underground in coal mines. Yet the 1920s were a watershed in a much broader sense; there were changing notions of femininity associated with new nationalist doctrines and a transformation of working class politics as a consequence of the rise of trade unions. In the realm of culture, nationalist discourse about women emphasised their duty as mothers rather than as wage earners. Female workers in mills, mines and factories, many of whom had acquired a reputation for militancy, also became the victims of economic rationalisation. Rather than seeking to extend their protection to working class women, the nascent Indian trade unions interpreted both their participation in the labour market and their resistance to the terms set by employers as a reason to exclude them from organised industrial relations. Sen concludes: 'The interests of management, faced with spiralling cost of labour, and unions, operating in a labour surplus economy, converged towards a masculinisation of organised labour' [255: 115].

Luise White was another pioneer of a gendered approach to labour history but she took it in a different direction from Sen by investigating 'writing about the colonial world with the images and idioms produced by the subjects themselves' [257: 29]. This necessitated an exploration of masculinity as well as femininity. On this basis White offered a new examination of African discourse about vampires using the stories she was told by elderly labourers and artisans in the late 1980s. These were tales that African working men shared among themselves. Aside from this gendered aspect of vampire myths, White's examination emphasised the significance of cultural narratives in constructing a hierarchy of labour: 'skilled labor portrayed itself and is portrayed in words of privilege and superiority' [257: 37]. When representing themselves and their work, artisans paraded their knowledge of, for example, the complex system of waterpipes which had to be mastered in order to perform effectively as a firefighter; when interpreted by others, this technical mastery or mechanical expertise often acquired a supernatural character. White found that the veiled interiors of the vehicles used by firefighters and policemen were widely regarded as sinister locations, the purpose of which was the extraction of blood from those who had been captured within them. On her account, other than the vampire idiom 'no other idea could carry the weight of the complications of work, identities and machines' [257: 41]. The prevalence of debates between Africans who proclaimed the existence of colonial vampires and those sceptics who rejected this mythology was intrinsically tied to apprehensions about modern forms of labour and technology introduced at the end of empire. In dealing with medical and legal aspects of African history, White later extended her scholarly range but her early work illustrates one means by which labour history, which has often been tied to objective measures of employment, wages and production, can be reconciled to postcolonial studies, when it emphasises the significance of discourses of gender and race.

Female Indian coal miners and male African firefighters operated in a market for their services, but many workers in the periphery were coerced into undertaking tasks which were essential to the maintenance of the colonial economy and their stories resonate into the present. Much recent work on African slavery is influenced by the continental perspective pioneered by Paul Lovejoy in the 1980s. While emphasising the impact that Islamic and Atlantic slavetraders had on the coasts, he suggested that indigenous African forms of slavery were more extensive and sophisticated than has sometimes been acknowledged by Western historians [250]. The persistence of African slaveholding traditions is emphasised by Beverly Grier and Kwabena Akurang-Parry whose investigations reveal the centrality of female servitude to capital accumulation in the Gold Coast and then Ghana during the 20th century. Grier suggests that the profitability of cocoa production was dependent on various forms of arduous unwaged female labour including not only the harvesting, drying and fermenting of beans but also their porterage, which was necessary to transport the beans before effective road and rail communications were established. Domestic labour might be thought to exist at some distance removed from rural cocoa production but the pawning of daughters and nieces in order to secure loans or relieve the indebtedness of fathers and uncles was an intrinsic element of the colonial economy. These patriarchal systems, which facilitated productivity and profitability, were, as Grier demonstrates, tolerated by the British authorities under the system of indirect rule [246]. In her later work, Grier went on to examine the central and overlooked role of child labour in the economic system of Southern Rhodesia [247].

Grier's West African work was largely corroborated by Akurang-Parry, who suggested that 'female and child forced labor contributed immensely to the early 20th century colonial economy' [236: 43]. He stresses the continuity and centrality of a form of unfree female domestic labour known as *abaawa*, across the pre-colonial, colonial and postcolonial periods. In Akan, *abaawa* denotes 'a prepubescent female or maiden' but in Ghana it has come to describe the status of a domestic servant who lives in the house in which she works. Historically, *abaawa* was sustained by the pawning of young girls who acted as involuntary labourers in upper- and middle-class households in return for the credit facilities made available to their male relatives. Although the colonial authorities expressed disapproval of such practices, Akurang-Parry suggests '*abaawa* became the most convenient form of cheap involuntary labor and, disguised as apprenticeship, was often excluded from the spectrum of anti-slavery, anti-forced labor proclamations of the 1920s and 1930s' [236: 31]. Due to the interest which the colonial authorities had in suppressing information about it, the number of women and girls subject to this form of coercion is, Akurang-Parry admits, difficult to estimate but oral testimonies suggest a reduction rather than a termination of *abaawa* in the late colonial period. This West African trade in female unfree labour continues to the present day [237].

Akurang-Parry's work illustrates the role of the colonial authorities in concealing evidence that girls and women were being compelled to work. This was an issue which mattered to British policymakers because opposition to unfree labour was an essential component of the ideology which justified late European imperialism. Cooper suggests that free labour was 'a vital concept distinguishing the progressive colonizer of the early twentieth century from the freebooters, bandits, kidnappers and buyers of human flesh who had for past centuries represented Europe overseas' [241: xx]. The extension of Britain's imperial reach with the acquisition of mandated territories from the defunct German and Ottoman empires after 1918 was underpinned by the ideology of free labour. Kevin Grant suggests that imperial expansion was justified to domestic and international audiences on the basis of its purportedly humanitarian character. When extending imperial reach into regions previously claimed by Berlin it was useful for British statesmen to point to the contrast between their commitment to policies of free labour and the disreputable behaviour of the African territories' erstwhile German governors. He quotes Alice Harris of the Anti-Slavery Society on this topic: 'The cardinal principle of British colonization is that of sacrifice and service, whereas that of the other powers has been primarily and very largely colonization in the material interests of the motherland' [244: 142]. The rhetoric employed was now that of a 'sacred trust', and among the obligations of trusteeship was the protection of workers from exploitation. British diplomats played a prominent role in codifying these obligations during the drafting of the League of Nations' Slavery Convention of 1926 and the United Nations' Supplementary Slavery Convention of 1956. Beneath the surface of this edifying regulatory regime, Grant suggests, matters were considerably murkier. As one of the leading metropolitan critics of empire, E.D. Morel, pointed out, the inter-war system of trusteeship was a means 'to reconcile the altruistic pronouncements of President Wilson with what is substantially a policy of imperialistic grab at the expense of a beaten foe' [245: 88]. The work of Suzanne Miers, which covers the whole of the 20th century, is continuous with that of Grant in illustrating the way in which debates over the 1956 UN Supplementary Convention on the Abolition of Slavery became an exercise in Cold War points scoring [251].

There continues to be a lively historiographical discussion about the colonial labour policies of the European states after 1918. Beyond the issues of international justification, the ambiguities which attended the definitions of free, forced and slave labour enabled the perpetuation of unfree labour. Opolot Okia contends that, even though official British policy disavowed forced labour, in Kenya it continued under the guise of traditional communal work. On his account, the undercapitalisation of European businesses in Africa and the financial impecunity of the colonial state created a structural problem which could only be resolved by the use of forced and low wage labour. It was the coercion of workers which guaranteed the profitability of privately owned plantations and mines, and enabled the state to maintain transport infrastructure at minimal expense. The Conservative Colonial Secretary, Leo Amery, was reluctant to authorise the use of forced labour to extend the Uganda railway in 1925 but acquiesced in the conscription of workers when it became evident that too few local Africans had volunteered. Once rising anti-slavery sentiment in Britain precluded the coercion of individuals, the problem was resolved by reinventing the tradition of communal labour as an inescapable obligation to work for the state. The hard labour involved in maintaining roads, railways and irrigation systems was often undertaken by women and children, in order to allow African men to engage in low paid wage-labour. Much of Okia's evidence on the use of violence to discipline communal labourers comes from the testimony of an archdeacon of the Church Missionary Society, Walter Owen, whose reports were hotly contested by British administrators. Further work is required to map more accurately the frontier between forced and free labour in inter-war Africa [253].

Although they were turned to national purposes, the campaigns against slavery and forced labour constitute interesting examples of the transnational exchange of ideas: opposition to these practices spread across the frontiers of states, often propelled forward by actors rooted in civil society and inspired by universalist ideas, most obviously by Christianity. However, as the work of Samita Sen indicates, the discussion of colonial labour politics can only proceed so far before exploring the connections between ideas and institutions, and this necessitates consideration of the key institutional manifestation of organised labour, the trade union [255]. During the 20th century millions of people in both the colonial metropolis and periphery joined unions but the impact this had on decolonisation is often dealt with only glancingly in accounts of the struggle for independence. One important exception is the work of Mary Chamberlain, whose interest in migration from the Caribbean led her to explore the connections between the Caribbean diaspora and the rise of labour protests on the Anglophone islands during the inter-war period. She found that it was not just the influence of famous Caribbean expatriates such as Marcus Garvey and George Padmore which promoted anti-colonial labour protest. Even before trade unions had a secure legal framework in which to operate, groups such as the Working Men's Association in Barbados began the process of organising workers on the islands. A host of lesser known figures such as the Guianese editor of the *West Africa Telegraph*, E.M. Hercules, and the Barbadian merchant seaman, Donald Moore, who had experience of labour militancy on the Clyde, travelled widely within and outside the Caribbean; in doing so, they propagated the notion that workers could improve their circumstances through the establishment of workers' organisations [129]. Chamberlain's extended analysis of the end of empire in Barbados encompasses not just themes of transnational activism and labour organisation but also the role of gender and other cultural forces in shaping nation-building in the Caribbean at the end of empire [20].

The role of British unions and the Trades Union Congress (TUC) in urging colonial workers to imitate British organisational models of industrial relations, was tackled 30 years ago by Marjorie Nicholson, who was a member of the TUC's international department [252]. Her work was sympathetic to the metropolitan perspective and focused on evidence of institutional collaboration between the emergent unions of the periphery and established metropolitan unions. More recently, Mary Davis has offered a shorter but more critical overview which argues that metropolitan unions, and the wider British labour movement, were excessively conservative in their approach to organising workers in the colonies. Preoccupied with concerns about racial conflict and communist subversion, British unions were anxious above all else to secure industrial peace in the colonies. Davis provides striking evidence of this tendency in the form of the pamphlets which the TUC provided as industrial relations primers. One guide for Kenya entitled *What is a Trade Union?* explained: 'Trade unions are formed so that strikes can be avoided. Trade unions try to make sure workers and employers understand one another ... The value of a worker to his employers depends on the kind of work he does ... good hard work is of more value than bad, lazy work' [243: 101].

It is the transnational activities of those large labour confederations with a global reach which is emerging as a particularly important area of study. During the 1990s Anthony Carew conducted pioneering research on the colonial consequences of the conflicts within the International Confederation of Free Trade Unions (ICFTU). The ICFTU was formed in 1949, when European and American unions split from the World Federation of Trade Unions (WFTU) on the grounds that the latter was increasingly dominated by communists. Subsequently, the two internationals competed for the affiliation of nascent colonial unions. Arguments over strategy broke out inside the ICFTU and it is these which Carew anatomised. The British TUC grew ever more critical of the 'fundamental unsoundness' of the efforts of the ICFTU's American affiliates to apply their own ideas about industrial relations to the colonies. For Carew such disagreements reflected different priorities: British trade union leaders did not regard communism as a realistic threat in African conditions and feared that the new unions on the continent would fall 'under the domination of governments and nationalist political movements as had already happened in Ghana' [239: 159]. By contrast, the overwhelming concern of the American unions and the ICFTU bureaucracy was to prevent the WFTU from establishing a communist presence in the colonial periphery and thus dragging African and Asian workers towards the Eastern Bloc in the Cold War. Aside from practical questions, such as who should train colonial trade union organisers, Carew suggests that transatlantic harmony was jeopardised by ideological differences and personality clashes, most of which centred on the former American communist, turned zealous anti-communist, Jay Lovestone. Efforts by Lovestone's Free Trade Union Committee to purge left wing activists from the global trade union movement divided the ICFTU between factions and culminated in the resignation of its Dutch secretary-general, J. H. Oldenbroek. Carew concludes that this schism had significant ramifications: 'it undermined the authority of labour's voice in international affairs, diminishing the standing of the organization that sought, on behalf of the largest group of workers in the non-communist world, to represent the values of trade unionism to the international community at large' [240: 177–178].

Partly because of the historiographical interest in Lovestone's career, for which there is no British equivalent, there is probably now a larger literature on the role of the American Federation of Labor – Congress of Industrial Organizations (AFL-CIO) in decolonisation than of the British TUC. The activities of Lovestone's acolytes, such as William Howard McCabe, Maida Springer and George Weaver, have received most coverage. As the only British colony on the American mainland, British Guiana has attracted the attention of Stephen Rabe, Robert Waters and Gordon Daniels. They have revealed how American labour activists, including McCabe, promoted industrial strife in the colony as a means of securing the removal of the territory's Marxist-inclined Chief Minister, Cheddi Jagan [204; 212]. Such interventions were greeted with dismay by British trade unionists and colonial bureaucrats. Similar patterns of transatlantic tension have been uncovered by Yevette Richards, who has utilised oral history testimony to explore some of the cultural foundations of British resistance to the presence of American trade unionists in the colonies. Her work focuses on the life of Maida Springer, who began her career as an official of the International Ladies' Garment Workers' Union and after 1945 became an envoy of the American Federation of Labour overseas. Her involvement in training East African trade unionists evoked the resentment of British colonial officialdom during the late 1950s [254].

According to Richards, some of this hostility derived from straightforward political considerations: it was believed that American labour officials would foster nationalism and anti-colonial militancy inside nascent African trade unions. But cultural forces were also at work. Springer's testimony, which is largely endorsed by Richards, is that considerations of race and gender were significant. It was not merely her sympathy for the liberationist aims of East African trade unionists that alarmed British officialdom, but her status as an influential black woman that guaranteed her a hostile reception from Colonial Office representatives in Africa. Recalling that the wife of a colonial governor had prevented her speaking to a meeting of the International Council of Women, Springer commented: 'I was not the kind of American person that a colonial government would look kindly on. I looked like every other African ... My very presence created hostility with the colonial government.'[1] For their part the leaders of the American trade union movement were conscious that African-American labour envoys would have an advantage in securing the allegiance of African and Asian trade unionists. The activities of the AFL-CIO official George Weaver in Singapore have been described by S. R. Joey Long as an example of adroit racial politics: 'US policymakers were shrewd in determining that an African-American would be more acceptable to local workers who might otherwise have been suspicious of American representatives' [249: 348].

Despite this increasing interest in the transnational manoeuvrings of Western trade unionists, large regions of the empire remain uncharted historiographical territory for labour historians. In a vein of self-recrimination, since writing *British Policy in Aden and the Protectorates* I have been struck by the way the book largely ignores the industrial struggle which played a seminal role in the rise of nationalism in the colony [26]. Perhaps the most significant episode was the introduction of an Industrial Relations Ordinance in 1960 which, by banning strike action under a wide range of circumstances, effectively reversed previous efforts to liberalise trade union laws in the colonies. The imposition of mandatory arbitration by an industrial court led to the jailing of union leaders. The cause of the local Aden Trade Union Congress (ATUC) was taken up by labour activists overseas. In its contest with the colonial authorities, ATUC drew on its alliances within the ICFTU to challenge restrictions on trade union rights. The head of the ICFTU's economic and social department, Alfred Braunthal, complained to the governor of Aden, William Luce, that the legislation was 'unique in the British overseas territories' and that 'the ICFTU could not accept the necessity for such legislation except in time of war'.[2] In this spirit the ICFTU sponsored a series of complaints to the International Labour Organisation (ILO) about the conduct of industrial relations in Aden. Such interventions were motivated less by the injustices of the legislation than by the ICFTU's rivalry with the WFTU and the fear that disillusioned workers in the colonies would turn to the Eastern bloc for assistance if none was forthcoming from the west. From the perspective of the ICFTU it was essential to nurture the ATUC and other non-communist unions in the colonies, as Cold War allies. By contrast colonial officials on the ground argued that the use of unions to pursue nationalist grievances was illegitimate. Events in Aden suggest that historians should take greater cognisance of the fact that labour disputes within particular colonies were enmeshed with ongoing competition between globalised trade union blocs. In such cases Cold War strategising was often misaligned with plans for orderly decolonisation.

If the Cold War implications of labour disputes have sometimes been neglected, historians have been more assiduous in tracking the impact of the colonial state's efforts to contain industrial militancy in the periphery. In his recent study of the strikes organised by the Workers' Affairs Association in Sudan, Gareth Curless notes that labour disputes at ports and railways became a feature of industrial relations in Africa during the 1940s. The preconditions for successful union organising were urbanisation and the emergence of a new class of skilled artisanal workers in permanent employment. Curless identifies the prime causes of the Sudan railway strikes of 1947–1948 as price inflation, inequities in pay and benefits, and the malfunctioning of the local Labour Board. Some improvements in conditions were obtained but the primary effect of the strikes, Curless argues, was to force a complacent imperial administration to recognise the necessity for a properly functioning trade union movement [242]. In the case of Kenyan coffee estates, David Hyde found that new trade unions were barely able to contain labour militancy. The general context for the 'avalanche of plantation strikes' which commenced in 1960 was the withdrawal of governmental support for plantation agriculture and the instability in world markets caused by the 'gargantuan stockpiles' of Brazilian and Columbian coffee. More significant still was the return to the labour market of radicalised Kikuyu detainees in the aftermath of the Mau Mau war. For those workers who had previously been fighters, including over 12,000 people in Thika district who participated in 42 strikes in early 1960, the struggle for improved working conditions was a continuation of their war with the colonial state [248].

Strikes were also turning points in independence campaigns. In his assessment of the Caribbean labour rebellions of the 1930s, Nigel Bolland suggests they were even more significant for the region's history than the emancipation of the slaves. They certainly revealed the coercive character of the colonial state and Bolland examines the role of police and volunteer forces who were deployed to confront the strikers; they 'were not only the frontline of protection for colonial property arrangements and social institutions, they were also the embodiment of racial privileges and hierarchy, which were maintained through violence' [238]. Bolland argues that the authoritarian features of the colonial state were inherited by the postcolonial governments of the region who have failed in their project of establishing a more egalitarian society. Martin Thomas corroborates and extends Bolland's findings in his own study of European colonial policing. He suggests that colonial supervision of industrial relations was not just a question of demanding good conduct but of the application of coercion to control labour. More tellingly still, he argues that 'the colonial protests which took up most police time after 1918 were more industrial than political in origin' [256: 325]. Such conclusions point once again to the requirement to investigate the changing relationship between labour and capital if we are to understand both imperial decline and the rise of new nation states in Asia, Africa and the Americas.

Conclusions

Having begun this historiographical survey by examining what the literature has to say about the ideas underpinning anti-colonialism, it is useful to end with a reminder that historians are also concerned with the material circumstances in which decolonisation occurred. Scholars of labour and business have uncovered evidence of the links between economics and politics in the operations of the sterling zone and the spread of trade unionism. In light of the Cain and Hopkins thesis, historians have come to regard the sterling area as a means of securing Britain's financial viability at a time when political independence for the periphery appeared imminent [216; 217; 223; 224]. On the labour side of the productive equation, the organising activities of trade unions were intended to facilitate orderly decolonisation by channelling the discontent of workers into a manageable industrial relations framework. But scholars have not simply regarded these institutions as a means of reconciling interests. In many instances conflict spilled over into politics: business priorities were often ordered differently from those of the state, while workers' protests and strikes were frequently resolved by violence. Furthermore, as the work of Grant on the free labour ideology of British imperialism or White's on the salience of vampire myths in Africa illustrates, labour history is not just a matter of re-examining the economic circumstances in which industrial relations took place; it also requires some consideration of wider ideological questions [244; 257].

Business and labour historians are also well placed to make a contribution to debates about decolonisation as a transnational phenomenon by examining both these new ideological currents and the movements of capital across national and imperial frontiers. These considerations return us to the notion of historical research as a cooperative enterprise. Although the Cain and Hopkins thesis inevitably received criticism, what was most striking was that its ideas could be tested by historians with specialisms in different regions and time periods [214; 220]. The result of their collective endeavour was a different and more persuasive account of the role of financial interests in British imperial history. The study of labour relations has tended to proceed in a more piecemeal fashion but key themes have been established including the importance of gender to an adequate understanding of the operations of colonial labour; the significance of coercion, which connects the history of labour to that of insurgency in the periphery; and the trilateral relationship between new forms of industrial relations, decolonisation and the Cold War. The largeness and significance of these issues ought to keep historians occupied for decades to come; but by way of a final conclusion it may be useful to offer a brief audit of the achievements of the most recent generation of scholars of British decolonisation.

Conclusion

One of the consequences of the end of the British Empire has been a tidal wave of commentary about the end of the British Empire. What this book has attempted to demonstrate is that this scholarly inundation has been beneficial and that we now have a better understanding of the character, causes and consequences of decolonisation. Two developments have been particularly significant in this process: firstly a revised interpretation of the decolonisation strategy pursued by the British government which emphasises the activism of the imperial state during the last years of empire and secondly a new and revisionary reading of decolonisation as a global process which paid no respect to the arbitrary and artificial frontiers that marked out nations and empires on the map. To the extent that the former emphasises the significance of outward pressure from the metropolis into the periphery and the latter accentuates the role of exogenous, global processes in shaping imperial history, these two interpretations are in tension with one another. Even as they offer a new depiction of the actions of the British government and its representatives overseas, traditional historians in the activist camp still rely on orthodox assumptions about the central role of an elite group of policymakers. On the other side of the divide, although a number of historians who have taken an interest in globalisation, such as John Darwin and Antony Hopkins, retain a foothold in the traditional camp, others are eager to press ahead with a complete reconceptualisation of decolonisation in order to place historical actors and ideas, that had been marginalised in traditional accounts, at the centre of the historical stage. The theoretical difficulties in reconciling these philosophical positions ought not to be underestimated but some authors have engaged with both. Although we have not had the 'full-fledged critical dialogue between the two parties' which Dane Kennedy called for 20 years ago, in practice, some interesting work has occurred when historians have synthesised these approaches [10]. Examples include Barbara Bush's account of the rise of anti-colonialism in Africa and Bill Schwarz's analysis of the impact of race and gender on metropolitan debates about imperialism [19: 114].

This endorsement of individual texts and the generally positive assessment of the current state of the historiography might invite scepticism, particularly at a time when modish attacks on the guild mentality of the British professional classes seem to grip the popular imagination ever more tightly. In an age when sceptics insist that no one should 'mark their own homework' it might be argued that it is unsurprising that a member of the cosy historians' academy should produce a laudatory appraisal of the literature in their own field. A critique of this kind can draw force from two observations, one more cynical than the other. The first, and less interesting, is that it would be an indictment of the academy if hundreds of historians working across a period of 25 years on the same subject matter were unable to demonstrate some evidence of scholarly progress. The second and perhaps more serious charge is that what looks like progress is more like a fetishisation of novelty in which the ever increasing demands made on historians to demonstrate the relevance and potency of their work require them to revise and innovate even where revision and innovation are unnecessary.

In ordinary parlance, the response to the first charge is that the historiography is more than the sum of its parts. Some historical sub-fields and even whole disciplines can fall into sterility and irrelevance when large numbers of scholars find themselves working on a narrowing range of problems with ever less interesting results. What this book has hopefully demonstrated is that the opposite has happened with the study of British decolonisation: recent writing in this field demonstrates the rich scholarly rewards which can accrue through the application of historical methods. It is perfectly possible for an army of academics to produce work which is uniform and mundane but the historiography on decolonisation is plural and fertile with new ideas. Uncovering new evidence from the past is often regarded as the quintessential historical activity and, for those committed to empiricism, the discovery of the Hanslope Park archive ought to qualify as confirmation of the vitality of the field. In addition, historians and archivists have generated new evidence in the form of oral histories, such as those that underpinned Urvashi Butalia's original account of the partition of India or Caroline Elkins's revisionist analysis of the Mau Mau insurgency [126; 166]. The historiography has also benefitted from the fact, which was noted in the introduction, that historians do not work in isolated silos: history remains a dialogue or conversation about the past. The exchanges and responses to the work of Peter Cain and Antony Hopkins on gentlemanly capitalism demonstrate how fruitful this can be [213; 220]. Perhaps more controversial might be the notion, which has featured strongly in this book, that the historiography should and does reflect present-day concerns; but it seems evident that the vitality of the scholarly literature on decolonisation is also a consequence of the willingness of historians to engage with the intellectual problems of the present in a way that acknowledges continuities and discontinuities. It is doubtful whether John Newsinger's work on counterinsurgency or Ama Biney's on the legacy of Kwame Nkrumah's career would be so compelling if they were not using the controversies of contemporary politics as inspiration for the investigation of the past [36; 180].

Still more contentious for some might be the suggestion that overt theorising has impinged on the historiography in a beneficial way. The apprehensions of many narrative historians about such developments also underpin the second potential criticism: that innovation can take priority over careful scholarship. It is worth noting that the obverse is also true: history would soon become a very dull discipline if confined to the endless rehearsal of orthodoxy. A thoroughgoing reappraisal of British imperial history, such as that undertaken by Cain and Hopkins, requires both a commitment to sustained research and the expenditure of a great deal of intellectual energy [216; 217]. On occasions, the critics of such large enterprises seem engaged in a futile attempt to bring down the elephant of revisionism with the peashooter of trivial counter-example. This does not imply that revisionist history ought to be immune from criticism and the balance of advantage ought to be judged on a case-by-case basis. Gerold Krozewski's qualified criticisms of the application of Cain and Hopkins's ideas to the period of decolonisation might be regarded as a model in that regard [224].

The most significant of all these controversies has taken place between purveyors of new imperial history, who have embraced ideas emanating from poststructuralism and postcolonialism, and defenders of traditional methodology, who are sceptical about revisionist history, particularly if it entails the importation of scholarly goods from other disciplines. The arguments which accompanied the publication of Bernard Porter's *Absent-Minded Imperialists* are of this order [111]. Although differences in the questions asked and the standards to which the two sides wish to appeal may appear so large as to make any kind of final adjudication impossible, once one examines the work produced under this new dispensation, it is difficult to gainsay the notion that, by considering new kinds of evidence and interpreting it in new ways, the new imperial history has enriched our understanding of decolonisation. In particular, the case for interrogating gender and race seems overwhelming. It is not necessary to agree with every nuance of Kathleen Paul's analysis of the racial impulses which underpinned British immigration policy or endorse all of Wendy Webster's conclusions about the influence of gender on modern notions of English identity, in order to acknowledge that their work marks a significant advance [119: 145]. But inevitably, the application of postcolonial ideas to the history of the end of empire are not always successful and with the tide running so strongly in its favour the risk of overcompensation and the fetishisation of novelty arises. Karl Hack has highlighted the danger of this revisionist over-compensation in the study of Britain's later imperial wars, while Ronald Hyam has made the case for revisiting the achievements of established schools of historiography in his survey of Britain's declining empire [9; 171].

This brings us finally to the question of the possibly illusory character of historiographical progress. Ten years ago, Stephen Howe sounded a cautionary note when examining the impact of the new imperial history upon our understanding of the domestic consequences of the ending of the British imperial project. He suggested that 'we are still groping around in an historiographical half-light on these themes' [73: 304]. In doing so he consciously invoked the most famous aphorism of the most famous philosopher of history, G.W.F. Hegel. In the preface to his *Philosophy of Right*, which argues that the past unfolds to reveal a pattern of progress, Hegel remarked: 'The Owl of Minerva spreads its wings only at the falling of the dusk.' At the risk of trampling over the many complexities and imponderables of Hegelian theory, and on the understanding that the 'Owl of Minerva' represents wisdom or understanding and that the 'falling of the dusk' is analogous to the termination of a particular historical era, this implies that historians may be in a better position to understand imperial decline now that the British Empire is no more. Interpreted in this way Hegel's notion has some resonance for students of contemporary historiography: scholars are unable to acquire an adequate understanding of one period of history, such as the era of European imperialism, while still living through it; only once it has been succeeded by a new epoch and become the past, does the possibility of a new and more accurate appraisal become feasible. The perplexities and lack of perspective with which we confront contemporary political and social problems certainly lend this thought a degree of credence, but with regard to the investigation of the imperial past Hegel's aphorism is doubly suggestive. On the one hand, now that posterior or retrospective judgement is possible, one would expect a lively debate based on the uncovering of new evidence and a fresh, critical examination of old perspectives. But, on the other, and given that the final demise of the British Empire is sometimes dated to the handover of Hong Kong to China less than two decades ago, one might also conclude that, having taken flight, the owl of Minerva is still on the wing: our understanding is still incomplete and there is more to do.

Chronology

In the age of Wikipedia a conventional march through a list of independence dates is redundant. This chronology therefore comprises a list of events which have some significance in the history of anti-colonialism, the culture and politics of empire in Britain, migration, late imperial warfare, propaganda and intelligence, and the impact of labour and capital in the British empire.

March 1919 Contrary to the expectations of British intelligence, a rebellion breaks out in Egypt in protest at the deportation of a number of nationalist leaders, including Saad Zaghlul.

April 1919 The massacre of unarmed protestors at Jallianwala Bagh in Amritsar discredits British imperial authority in India and provokes further disturbances across the Punjab.

April 1920 At San Remo, the victorious allied powers agree that the Arab provinces of the Ottoman Empire will become League of Nations mandates; under these terms, Britain subsequently acquires responsibility for the administration of Iraq, Transjordan and Palestine.

May 1922 The Empire Settlement Act establishes the basis for state-supported migration by white Britons to the dominions, which continues in various forms until 1972.

February 1925 The British government endorses the conscription of labour for work on extending the Uganda railway.

March 1925 The Special Restriction (Coloured Alien Seamen) Order initiates an official campaign of harassment directed against black seamen in Britain's port cities.

September 1926 British diplomats play an influential role in the drafting of the Slavery Convention, prohibiting chattel slavery, which is passed by the League of Nations Assembly.

June 1928 Legislation is introduced in India which bans women from underground work in coal mines.

March 1930 Gandhi and his supporters begin a march to the sea in protest against the Indian Government's monopoly over salt production.

September 1930 Labour's Colonial Secretary, Lord Passfield, issues a memorandum advising colonial governments to provide a legal framework for the operation of trade unions.

June 1931 The Security Service (MI5) is given responsibility for collecting intelligence within the British Empire.

August 1932 A series of bilateral agreements are made at the end of the Ottawa Conference which introduce a system of imperial preference in international trade.

August 1935 The Government of India Act, establishing a degree of provincial autonomy in the country, is passed following a long series of domestic controversies in Britain.

April 1936 The Arab revolt in Palestine begins with a strike in Nablus; for the next three years the British pioneer many of the punitive counter-insurgency tactics that characterise late imperial warfare, in an effort to contain the rebellion.

May 1938 Disturbances at the docks in Kingston escalate into a labour insurrection in Jamaica requiring the despatch of a British warship. Violence across the Anglophone Caribbean prompts a new focus on economic development and industrial relations reform in British colonial policy.

August – November 1939 A series of amendments to the Defence (Finance) Regulations formalise and extend the emergent sterling area, which is regulated by the free exchange of currency inside the area and new restrictions on financial transfers outside it.

July 1940 The Colonial Development and Welfare Act is promulgated and establishes the basis for new programmes of financial assistance to the colonies after the Second World War.

November 1944 Eric Williams publishes *Capitalism and Slavery* which constitutes the first salvo in his assault on the purportedly humanitarian character of British imperial reform.

March 1947 Communal violence inside India spreads to Lahore and Amritsar and leads to a transformation in the demography of both cities in the months before independence.

March 1947 The UK-Australia Free and Assisted Passage scheme becomes operative and subsidises the migration of the 'Ten Pound Poms' to Australia.

July 1947 Sterling is briefly made convertible but currency restrictions are almost immediately reimposed to end the outflow of capital from the sterling area.

October 1947 The Exchange Control Act formalises the rules governing currency payments by the territories of the sterling area.

June 1948 The Malayan Communist Party under the direction of Chin Peng launches an insurgency against British rule in Malaya.

June 1948 Disembarkation of Caribbean migrants from the *Empire Windrush*, which is later identified as a symbolic moment in the rise of multi-cultural Britain.

June 1949 Kwame Nkrumah founds the Convention People's Party in the Gold Coast and outlines the tactics of 'Positive Action' which will lead to independence for the renamed Ghana eight years later.

July 1949 The British South Africa Company negotiates a deal to relinquish royalty payments on its profitable Northern Rhodesian mining rights in 1986; the rights are actually returned to the Zambian government at independence in 1964.

December 1949 The Abducted Persons (Recovery and Restoration Act) is passed by the Indian parliament and requires women abducted during the partition violence to reunite with their families who had migrated to the Indian side of the Radcliffe frontier.

September 1950 The death of Jan Smuts initiates a parliamentary debate about how to commemorate one of the leading imperialists of the age and six years later leads to the unveiling of the statue of Smuts in Parliament Square.

May 1951 George VI declares the Festival of Britain open; its symbol is a modernist iteration of an image traditionally associated with imperialism – Britannia.

April 1953 The Lari massacre of Kenyan loyalists by Mau Mau adherents leads to reprisals including the execution of those convicted of the crime and the internment of many others in labour camps.

August 1953 The Central African Federation is established; its future remains a contentious issue in British and African politics for the next decade.

April 1955 The Templer Report on imperial security recommends the strengthening of intelligence organisation in Britain's remaining colonies.

November 1956 Prime Minister Anthony Eden agrees to a ceasefire which ends the short Suez war with Egypt and precipitates a major division within the Conservative Party.

March 1957 Ghana becomes the first sub-Saharan African state to become independent with Nkrumah as its first prime minister.

October 1957 At their annual conference in Brighton the Labour Party accepts that all colonial territories, irrespective of size, should obtain independence.

December 1958 Agreement is reached with overseas holders of sterling that the currency should be made fully convertible by amalgamating 'transferable' and 'dollar area' sterling accounts.

March 1959 The death of eleven internees at the Hola detention camp in Kenya leads to further scrutiny of the conduct of the colonial government's counter-insurgency campaign against the Mau Mau.

August 1960 A new Industrial Relations Ordinance is introduced in Aden which effectively reverses previous reforms by preventing unions from taking strike action.

April 1962 The first Commonwealth Immigrants Act is passed; it establishes a voucher system with the aim of restricting the entry of migrants from the Caribbean and South Asia.

September 1962 A Republican coup in Yemen provides an opportunity for British intelligence to sponsor subversion from across the imperial frontier in Aden under the codename RANCOUR.

December 1964 After the introduction of unprecedented electoral reforms which institute a system of proportional representation, Cheddi Jagan's People's Progressive Party are finally defeated in a Guianese election, thus paving the way for independence under Forbes Burnham.

October 1965 In response to an abortive coup by the Indonesian left, the British government curtails cross-border CLARET raids into Borneo, which facilitates the massacres of the military's opponents by the Indonesian army.

November 1965 The British Indian Ocean Territory [BIOT] is formed comprising islands previously administered as part of the colonial territories of the Seychelles and Mauritius.

January 1967 Duncan Sandys organises a Peace with Rhodesia rally in Trafalgar Square which culminates with fighting in Downing Street.

March 1968 A new Commonwealth Immigrants Act is passed which introduces the concept of patriality as a means of restricting immigration from East Africa.

April 1968 Enoch Powell's 'Rivers of Blood' speech predicts future racial conflict and elicits large scale protests against black migration to Britain.

September 1971 The last residents of Diego Garcia are transferred from the BIOT to Mauritius to facilitate the establishment of American military facilities on the island.

August 1972 Idi Amin announces his intention to expel the Asian population of Uganda; those with British passports are allowed to relocate to the United Kingdom.

March 1981 The Black People's Day of Action inspires a march through London in response to institutional failures in dealing with the Deptford fire.

December 1989 After years of obscurity the communist guerrilla, Chin Peng, reappears and signs a peace agreement with the Malaysian government. He subsequently begins work on a book, *Alias Chin Peng*, which gives his side of the history of the Malayan war.

July 1993 The Waldegrave Initiative on Open Government is embodied in a White Paper and leads to the gradual release of a large body of previously declassified material, including many Security Service papers relating to colonial affairs at the end of empire.

April 2011 The British government discloses the existence of an archive of secret material at Hanslope Park, much of which relates to the history of colonialism.

June 2013 British Foreign Secretary, William Hague, issues a statement of regret for the maltreatment of detainees during the Mau Mau insurgency and offers compensation to veterans of the war.

Bibliography

General

1. J. M. Brown, *Windows into the Past: Life Histories and the History of South Asia* (Notre Dame, 2008)
2. A. Burton, 'Getting Outside of the Global: Repositioning British Imperialism in World History' in C. Hall and K. McClelland (eds.), *Race Nation and Empire: Making Histories, 1750 to the Present* (Manchester, 2010), 199–216
3. D. Chakrabarty, *Provinicializing Europe: Postcolonial Thought and Historical Difference* (Princeton, 2000)
4. J. Darwin, *The Empire Project: The Rise and Fall of the British World System* (Cambridge, 2009)
5. J. Darwin, 'Globalism and Imperialism: The Global Context of British Power 1830–1960' in S. Akita (ed.), *Gentlemanly Capitalism, Imperialism and Global History* (Basingstoke, 2002), 43–64
6. C. Elkins, 'Alchemy of Violence: Mau Mau, the British Empire and the High Court of Justice', *Journal of Imperial and Commonwealth History* 39/5 (2011), 731–748
7. E. Hampshire, '"Apply the Flame More Searingly": The Destruction and Migration of the Archives of British Colonial Administration', *Journal of Imperial and Commonwealth History* 41/2 (2013), 334–352
8. A.G. Hopkins, 'Rethinking Decolonization', *Past and Present* 200 (2008), 211–247
9. R. Hyam, *Britain's Declining Empire* (Cambridge, 2006)
10. D. Kennedy, 'Imperial History and Post-Colonial Theory', *Journal of Imperial and Commonwealth History* 24/3 (1996), 345–363
11. K. Kyle, 'Suez and the Waldegrave Initiative', *Contemporary Record* 9/2 (1995), 378–393
12. Wm. R. Louis and R. Robinson, 'The Imperialism of Decolonization', *Journal of Imperial and Commonwealth History* 22/3 (1994), 462–511
13. J. M. MacKenzie, 'Irish, Scottish, Welsh and English Worlds? A Four Nations Approach to the History of the British Empire', *History Compass* 6/5 (2008), 1244–1263
14. S. Mawby, 'Orientalism and the Failure of British Policy in the Middle East', *History* 95/319 (2010), 332–353

15. D. Olusoga, *The World's War* (London, 2014)
16. V. Prashad, *The Darker Nations: A People's History of the Third World* (New York, 2008)

Regional and Country Studies

17. C. Bayly and T. Harper, *Forgotten Wars: The End of Britain's Asian Empire* (London, 2007)
18. J. Belich, *Paradise Reforged: A History of the New Zealanders from the 1880s to the year 2000* (Auckland, 2001)
19. B. Bush, *Imperialism, Race and Resistance: Africa and Britain 1919–1945* (London, 1999)
20. M. Chamberlain, *Empire and Nation-Building in the Caribbean: Barbados 1937–1966* (Manchester, 2010)
21. L. P. Chester, *Borders and Conflict in South Asia: The Radcliffe Boundary Commission and the Partition of Punjab* (Manchester, 2009)
22. T. Dodge, 'Iraq: The Contradictions of Exogenous State-Building', *Third World Quarterly* 27/1 (2006), 187–200
23. Y. Khan, *The Great Partition: The Making of India and Pakistan* (London, 2007)
24. D. Lowry, 'Rhodesia 1890–1980: "The Lost Dominion"' in R. Bickers (ed.), *Settlers and Expatriates: Britons over the Seas* (Oxford, 2010), 112–149
25. S. Mawby, *Ordering Independence: The End of Empire in the Anglophone Caribbean 1947–1969* (Basingstoke, 2012)
26. S. Mawby, *British Policy in Aden and the Protectorates* (Abingdon, 2005)
27. J. C. Parker, *Brother's Keeper: The United States, Race and Empire in the British Caribbean* (Oxford, 2008)
28. C. Polsgrove, *Ending British Rule in Africa* (Manchester, 2009)
29. A. I. Singh, *The Origins of the Partition of India* (Oxford, 1987)
30. S. Smith, *Ending Empire in the Middle East* (Abingdon, 2012)
31. S. Smith, 'Revolution and Reaction: South Arabia in the Aftermath of the Yemeni Revolution', *Journal of Imperial and Commonwealth History* 28/3 (2001), 193–208
32. I. Talbot and G. Singh, *The Partition of India* (Cambridge, 2009)

Anticolonialism

33. J. Adams, *Gandhi: Naked Ambition* (London, 2010)
34. J. M. Allman, 'The Youngmen and the Porcupine: Class, Nationalism and the Asante's Struggle for Self-Determination 1957–1957', *The Journal of African History* 31/2 (1990), 263–279
35. A. Biney, 'The Legacy of Kwame Nkrumah in Retrospect', *The Journal of Pan African Studies* 2/3 (2008), 129–159

36. A. Biney, *The Political and Social Thought of Kwame Nkrumah* (Basingstoke, 2011)
37. K. Boodhoo, *The Elusive Eric Williams* (Kingston, 2001)
38. G. R. Bosch Jr., 'Eric Williams and the Moral Rhetoric of Dependency Theory', *Callaloo* 20/4 (1997), 817–827
39. K. Botwe-Asamoah, *Kwame Nkrumah's Politico-Cultural Thought and Policies* (London, 2005)
40. S. Cudjoe, 'Eric Williams and the Politics of Language', *Callaloo* 20/4 (1997), 753–63
41. S. Cudjoe (ed.), *Eric E. Williams Speaks: Essays on Colonialism and Independence* (Amherst, 1993)
42. D. Dalton, *Mahatma Gandhi: Nonviolent Power in Action* (New York, 2012)
43. B. Davidson, *Black Star: A View of the Life and Times of Kwame Nkrumah* (London, 1973)
44. J. Derrick, *Africa's 'Agitators': Militant Anti-Colonialism in Africa and the West* (New York, 2008)
45. F. Devji, *The Impossible Indian: Gandhi and the Temptation of Violence* (London, 2012)
46. R. Guha, *Gandhi Before India* (London, 2013)
47. C. L. R. James, *Nkrumah and the Ghana Revolution* (London, 1977)
48. G. Lamming, 'The Legacy of Eric Williams', *Callaloo* 20/4 (1997), 731–736
49. J. Lelyveld, *Great Soul: Mahatma Gandhi and his Struggle with India* (New York, 2011)
50. C. Markovits, *The Un-Gandhian Gandhi: The Life and Afterlife of the Mahatma* (London, 2004)
51. T. Martin, 'Eric Williams and the Anglo American Caribbean Commission', *Journal of African-American History* 88/3 (2003)
52. S. Mawby, '"Uncle Sam, We Want Back We Land": Eric Williams and the Anglo-American Controversy over the Chaguaramas Base', *Diplomatic History* 36/1 (2012), 119–145
53. A. Mazrui, *Nkrumah's Legacy and Africa's Triple Heritage between Globalization and Counter Terrorism* (Accra, 2004)
54. P. Mishra, *From the Ruins of Empire: The Revolt Against the West and the Remaking of Asia* (London, 2012)
55. P. Mohammed, 'A Very Public Private Man' in A. Allahar (ed.), *Caribbean Charisma: Reflections on Leadership, Legitimacy and Populist Politics* (London, 2001), 155–191
56. M. Mukherjee, 'Transcending Identity: Gandhi, Nonviolence and the Pursuit of a "Different" Freedom in Modern India', *American Historical Review* 115/2 (2010), 453–473
57. C. A. Palmer, *Eric Williams and the Making of the Modern Caribbean* (Chapel Hill, 2006)
58. R. Rathbone, *Nkrumah and the Chiefs* (Oxford, 2000)
59. R. Rathbone, 'Casting "the Kingdome into another mold": Ghana's Troubled Transition to Independence', *The Round Table* 97/398 (2008), 705–718

60. D. Rothchild, 'Colonial Bargaining as Tactics: The Ghana Experience 1954–1957', *International Negotiation* 10 (2005), 211–234
61. S. Ryan, *Eric Williams, The Myth and the Man* (Kingston, 2009)
62. Y. Saaka, 'Recurrent Themes in Ghanaian Politics: Kwame Nkrumah's Legacy', *Journal of Black Studies* 24/3 (1994), 263–280
63. T. Sarkar, 'Gandhi and Social Relation' in J. M. Brown and Anthony J. Parel (eds.), *The Cambridge Companion to Gandhi* (Cambridge, 2011), 173–195
64. R. B. Sheridan, 'Eric Williams and Capitalism and Slavery' in Barbara Lewis Solow and Stanley L. Engerman (eds.), *British Capitalism and Caribbean Slavery: The Legacy of Eric Williams* (Cambridge, 1987), 317–345
65. A. J. Stockwell, 'Chin Peng and the Struggle for Malaya', *Journal of the Royal Asiatic Society of Great Britain & Ireland* (2006), 279–297
66. P. Sutton, 'The Historian as Politician: Eric Williams and Walter Rodney' in A. Hennessy (ed.), *Intellectuals in the Twentieth Century Caribbean Vol. 1* (London, 1992), 98–114
67. T. Weber, *Gandhi as Disciple and Mentor* (Cambridge, 2004)

Metropolitan Politcs

68. S. Ball, 'Banquo's Ghost: Lord Salisbury, Harold Macmillan and the High Politics of Decolonization 1957–1963', *Twentieth Century British History* 16/1 (2005), 74–102
69. R. Bunce and P. Field, *Darcus Howe: A Political Biography* (London, 2013)
70. N. Deakin, *Colour, Citizenship and British Society* (London, 1970)
71. R. S. Grayson, 'Imperialism in Conservative Defence and Foreign Policy: Leo Amery and the Chamberlains 1903–1939', *Journal of Imperial and Commonwealth History* 34/4 (2006), 505–527
72. S. Howe, *Anticolonialism in British Politics* (Oxford, 1993)
73. S. Howe, 'Internal Decolonization? British Politics Since Thatcher as Post-Colonial Trauma', *Twentieth Century British History* 14/3 (2003), 286–304
74. S. Howe, 'Labour and International Affairs' in D. Tanner, P. Thane and N. Tiratsoo (eds.), *Labour's First Century* (Cambridge, 2000), 119–150
75. L. James, *Churchill and Empire* (London, 2013)
76. P. Kelemen, 'Planning for Africa: The British Labour Party's Colonial Development Policy 1920–1964', *Journal of Agrarian Change* 7/1 (2007), 76–98
77. P. Kelemen, 'The British Labour Party and the Economics of Decolonization: The Debate Over Kenya', *Journal of Colonialism and Colonial History* 8/3 (2008)
78. Wm. R. Louis, *In the Name of God Go!: Leo Amery and the British Empire in the Age of Churchill* (New York, 1992)
79. A. M. Messina, *Race and Party Competition in Britain* (Oxford, 1989)
80. K. O. Morgan, *Callaghan: A Life* (Oxford, 1997)

81. K. O. Morgan, 'Imperialists at Bay: British Labour and Decolonization', *Journal of Imperial and Commonwealth History* 27/2 (1999), 233–254
82. A. Muldoon, *Empire, Politics and the Creation of the 1935 India Act* (Farnham, 2009)
83. P. Murphy, *Alan Lennox-Boyd: A Biography* (London, 1999)
84. P. Murphy, *Party Politics and Decolonization* (Oxford, 1995)
85. S. Onslow, '"Battlelines for Suez": The Abadan Crisis of 1951 and the Formation of the Suez Group', *Contemporary British History* 17/2 (2003), 1–28
86. S. Onslow, *Backbench Debate within the Conservative Party and its Influence on British Foreign Policy 1948–1957* (Basingstoke, 1997)
87. N. Owen, *The British Left and India: Metropolitan Anti-Imperialism* (Oxford, 2002)
88. N. Owen, 'The Conservative Party and Indian Independence 1945–1947', *Historical Journal* 46/2 (2003), 403–436
89. M. Pitchford, *The Conservative Party and the Extreme Right* (Manchester, 2011)
90. J. Ramsden, *The Age of Churchill and Eden 1940–1957* (London, 1995)
91. A. Seldon and S. Ball (eds.), *Conservative Century* (Oxford, 1994)
92. A. Sivanandan, 'Race, Economy and the State: The Political Economy of Immigration', *Race & Class* 17/4 (1976)
93. M. Steele, 'Labour and the Central African Federation: Paternalism, Partnership and Black Nationalism', in Billy Frank, Craig Horner and David Stewart (eds.), *The British Labour Movement and Imperialism* (Newcastle, 2010), 131–147
94. M. Stuart, 'A Party in Three Pieces: The Conservative Split Over Rhodesian Oil Sanctions', *Contemporary British History* 16/1 (2002), 51–88
95. R. Toye, *Churchill's Empire* (London, 2010)
96. C. Watts, 'Killing Kith and Kin: The Viability of British Military Intervention in Rhodesia 1964–1965', *Twentieth Century British History* 16/4 (2005), 382–415
97. R. C. Whiting, 'The Empire and British Politics' in A. Thompson (ed.), *Britain's Experience of Empire in the Twentieth Century* (Oxford, 2012), 161–210

Metropolitan Culture

98. J. Burkett, *Constructing Post-Imperial Britain: Britishness, 'Race' and the Radical Left in the 1960s* (Basingstoke, 2013)
99. A. Burton, *At the Heart of Empire: Indians and the Colonial Encounter in Late Victorian Britain* (1998)
100. A. Burton, 'Review: The Absent-Minded Imperialists', *Victorian Studies* 47/4 (2005), 626–628
101. B. Conekin, *'The Autobiography of a Nation': The 1951 Festival of Britain* (Manchester, 2003)
102. R. Gilmour and B. Schwarz (ed.), *End of Empire and the English Novel* (Manchester, 2011)

103. P. Gilroy, '"My Britain is Fuck All": Zombie Multiculturalism and the Race Politics of Citizenship', *Identities: Global Studies in Culture and Power* 19/4 (2012), 380–397
104. W. James, 'The Black Experience in Twentieth Century Britain' in P. D. Morgan and S. Hawkins (eds.), *Black Experience and the Empire* (Oxford, 2004), 347–386
105. K. Kenny (ed.), *Ireland and the British Empire* (Oxford, 2004)
106. K. Kumar, 'Empire, Nation and National Identities' in A. Thompson (ed.), *Britain's Experience of Empire in the Twentieth Century* (Oxford, 2012), 298–329
107. J. Littler, '"Festering Britain": The 1951 Festival of Britain, Decolonisation and the Representation of the Commonwealth' in S. Faulkner and A. Ramamurthy (eds.), *Visual Culture and Decolonisation in Britain* (Aldershot, 2008), 21–42
108. D. Lowry, 'Ulster Resistance and Loyalist Rebellion in the British Empire' in K. Jeffery (ed.), *An Irish Empire? Aspects of Ireland and the British Empire* (Manchester, 1996), 191–215
109. J. M. MacKenzie, *Propaganda and Empire: Manipulation of British Public Opinion 1880–1960* (Manchester, 1988)
110. J. M. MacKenzie (ed.), *Scotland and the British Empire* (Oxford, 2011)
111. B. Porter, *The Absent-Minded Imperialists: What the British Really Thought About Empire* (Oxford, 2004)
112. B. Porter, 'Further Thoughts on Imperial Absent-Mindedness', *Journal of Imperial and Commonwealth History* 36/1 (2008), 101–117
113. A. S. Rush, *Bonds of Empire: West Indians and Britishness from Victoria to Decolonization* (Oxford, 2011)
114. B. Schwarz, *The White Man's World: Memories of Empire Vol I* (Oxford, 2011)
115. B. Schwarz, 'Reveries of Race: The Closing of the Imperial Moment' in B. Conekin, F. Mort and C. Waters (eds.), *Moments of Modernity: Reconstructing Britain 1945–1964* (London, 1999), 189–207
116. A. Thompson, *The Empire Strikes Back? The Impact of Imperialism on Britain from the Mid-Nineteenth Century* (Harlow, 2005)
117. S. Ward, '"No Nation Could be Broker": The Satire Boom and the Demise of Britain's World Role' in S. Ward (ed.), *British Culture and the End of Empire* (Manchester, 2001), 91–110
118. S. Ward, 'Introduction' in S. Ward (ed.), *British Culture and the End of Empire* (Manchester, 2001), 1–20
119. W. Webster, *Englishness and Empire 1939–1965* (Oxford, 2005)

Migration

120. H. Adi, *West Africans in Britain 1900–1960: Nationalism, Pan-Africanism and Communism* (London, 1998)
121. J. Belich, *Replenishing the Earth: The Settler Revolution and the Rise of the Anglo World* (Oxford, 2009)
122. A. Bhalla, *Stories about the Partition of India* (Delhi, 1994)

Bibliography

123. R. Bickers (ed.), *Settlers and Expatriates: Britons over the Seas* (Oxford, 2010)
124. C. Bridge and K. Fedorowich (eds.), *The British World: Diaspora, Culture and Identity* (London, 2003)
125. P. Buckner and R. D. Francis (eds.), *Rediscovering the British World* (Calgary, 2005)
126. U. Butalia, *The Other Side of Silence: Voices from the Partition of India* (London, 1998)
127. B. Carter, 'Review: Citizenship and Immigration in Post-war Britain', *Ethnic and Racial Studies* 24/4 (2001), 662–664
128. D. Cesarani, 'Review: Whitewashing Britain', *English Historical Review* 114/459 (1999), 1384–1385
129. M. Chamberlain, 'Local Radicals Abroad: The View to and from the Caribbean in the 1920s and 1930s' in K. Cowman and I. Packer (eds.), *Radical Cultures and Local Identities* (Newcastle, 2010), 177–194
130. J. Chatterji, '"Dispersal" and the Failure of Rehabilitation: Refugee Camp-Dwellers and Squatters in West Bengal', *Modern Asian Studies* 41/5 (2007), 995–1032
131. S. Constantine, 'Introduction: Empire Migration and Imperial Harmony' in S. Constantine (ed.), *Emigrants and Empire: British Settlement in the Dominions between the Wars* (Manchester, 1990)
132. S. Constantine, 'Waving Goodbye? Australia, Assisted Passages and the Empire and Commonwealth Settlements Act 1945–1972' in P. Burroughs and A. J. Stockwell (eds.), *Managing the Business of Empire* (London, 1998), 176–195
133. S. Constantine, '"Dear Grace…Love Maidi": Interpeting a Migrant's Letters from Australia' in K. Fedorowich and Andrew S. Thompson (eds.), *Empire, Migration and Identity in the British World* (Manchester, 2013)
134. C. Coombs, 'Partition Narratives: Displaced Trauma and Culpability among British Civil Servants in 1940s Punjab', *Modern Asian Studies* 45/1 (2011), 201–224
135. K. Fedorowich, *Unfit for Heroes: Reconstruction and Soldier Settlement in the Empire Between the Wars* (Manchester, 1994)
136. G. Gmelch, *Double Passage: The Lives of Caribbean Migrants at Home and Abroad* (Ann Arbor, 1992)
137. Y. Hamai, '"Imperial Burden" or "Jews of Africa"? An Analysis of Political and Media Discourse in the Ugandan Asian Crisis', *Twentieth Century British History* 22/3 (2011), 415–436
138. A. J. Hammerton and A. Thomson, *Ten Pound Poms: Australia's Invisible Migrants* (Manchester, 2005)
139. A. J. Hammerton, '"I'm a citizen of the world": Late Twentieth Century British Emigration and Global Identities' in K. Fedorowich and Andrew S. Thompson (eds.), *Empire, Migration and Identity in the British World* (Manchester, 2013)
140. R. Hansen, *Citizenship and Immigration in Post-War Britain* (Oxford, 2000)
141. J. Herbert, 'The British Ugandan Asian Diaspora: Multiple and Contested Belongings', *Global Networks* 12/3 (2012), 296–313

142. N. S. Khan, 'Identity, Violence and Women: A Reflection on the Partition of India' in Nighat Said Khan (ed.), *Locating the Self: Perceptions on Women and Multiple Identities* (Lahore, 1994), 157–171

143. G. D. Khosla, *Stern Reckoning: A Survey of the Events Leading Up To and Following the Partition of India* (Oxford, 1989)

144. G. Pandey, '"Nobody's Fool": The Dalits of Punjab in the Forced Removal of 1947' in R. Bessel and C. B. Haake (eds.), *Removing Peoples: Forced Removals in the Modern World* (Oxford, 2009)

145. K. Paul, *Whitewashing Britain: Race and Citizenship in the Postwar Era* (Ithaca, 1997)

146. M. Phillips and T. Phillips, *Windrush: The Irresistible Rise of Multi-Racial Britain* (London, 1998)

147. E. Robertson, '"Green for Come": Moving to York as a Ugandan Asian Refugee' in P. Panayi and P. Virdee (eds.), *Refugees and the End of Empire: Imperial Collapse and Forced Migration in the Twentieth Century* (Basingstoke, 2011), 245–267

148. M. Roe, *Australia, Britain and Migration 1915–1940: A Study in Desperate Hopes* (Cambridge, 1995)

149. P. H. Sand, *The United States and Britain in Diego Garcia: The Future of a Controversial Base* (Basingstoke, 2009)

150. I. R. G. Spencer, *British Immigration Policy Since 1939: The Making of Multi-Racial Britain* (London, 1997)

151. L. Tabili, *'We Ask for British Justice': Workers and Racial Difference in Late Imperial Britain* (London, 1994)

152. I. Talbot, *Divided Cities: Partition and its Aftermath in Lahore and Amritsar 1947–1957* (Oxford, 2006)

153. A. Thompson and K. Fedorowich (eds.), *Empire, Migration and Identity in the British World* (Manchester, 2013)

154. D. Vine, *Island of Shame: The Secret History of the US Military Base in Diego Garcia* (Princeton, 2009)

155. J. Walvin, *Passage to Britain* (Harmondsworth, 1984)

156. K. Williams, '"A Way Out of Our Troubles": The Politics of Empire Settlement' in S. Constantine (ed.), *Emigrants and Empire: British Settlement in the Dominions between the Wars* (Manchester, 1990)

Insurgency and Counterinsurgency

157. D. Anderson, *Histories of the Hanged: Britain's Dirty War in Kenya and the End of Empire* (London, 2005)

158. D. Anderson, 'British Abuse and Torture in Kenya's Counter-Insurgency 1952–1960', *Small Wars and Insurgencies* 23/4–5 (2012), 700–719

159. H. Bennett, 'The Other Side of COIN: Minimum and Exemplary Force in British Army Counterinsurgency in Kenya', *Small Wars and Insurgencies* 18/4 (2007), 638–664

160. H. Bennett, 'Minimum Force in British Counterinsurgency', *Small Wars and Insurgencies* 21/3 (2010), 459–475

161. H. Bennett, '"A Very Salutary Effect": The Counter-Terror Strategy in the Early Malayan Emergency', *Journal of Strategic Studies* 32/3 (2009), 415–444

162. J. Blacker, 'The Demography of Mau Mau: Fertility and Mortality in Kenya in the 1950s', *African Affairs* 106/423, 205–227

163. D. Branch, *Defeating Mau Mau, Creating Kenya: Counterinsurgency, Civil War and Decolonization* (Cambridge, 2009)

164. S. Carruthers, 'Being Beastly to the Mau Mau', *Twentieth Century British History* 16/4 (2005), 89–496

165. A. Edwards, *Defending the Realm: The Politics of Britain's Small Wars Since 1945* (Manchester, 2012)

166. C. Elkins, *Imperial Reckoning: The Untold Story of Britain's Gulag in Kenya* (New York, 2005)

167. D. French, *The British Way In Counter-Insurgency* (Oxford, 2011)

168. D. French, 'Nasty Not Nice: British Counter-Insurgency Doctrine and Practice 1945–1967', *Small Wars and Insurgencies* 23/4–5 (2012), 744–761

169. B. Grob-Fitzgibbon, *Imperial Endgame: Britain's Dirty Wars and the End of Empire* (Basingstoke, 2011)

170. K. Hack, 'Screwing Down the People: The Malayan Emergency, Decolonisation and Ethnicity' in H. Antlöv and S. Tønnesson (eds.), *Imperial Policy and Southeast Asian Nationalism* (London, 1995)

171. K. Hack, 'Everyone Lived in Fear: Malaya and the British Way in Counter-insurgency', *Small Wars and Insurgencies* 23/4–5 (2012), 671–699

172. M. Hughes, 'Introduction: British Ways of Counter-insurgency', *Small Wars and Insurgencies* 23/4–5 (2012), 580–590

173. M. Hughes, 'The Banality of Brutality: British Armed Forces and the Repression of the Arab Revolt in Palestine 1936–1939', *English Historical Review* 124/507 (2009), 313–354

174. T. Mockaitis, 'The Origins of British Counter-Insurgency', *Small Wars and Insurgencies* 1/3 (1990), 209–225

175. T. Mockaitis, 'The Minimum Force Debate: Contemporary Sensibilities Meet Imperial Practice', *Small Wars and Insurgencies* 23/4–5 (2012), 762–780

176. T. Mockaitis, *British Counterinsurgency 1919–1960* (London, 1990)

177. T. Mockaitis, *British Counterinsurgency in the Post-imperial Era* (Manchester, 1995)

178. A. Mumford, *The Counter-Insurgency Myth: The British Experience of Irregular Warfare*

179. P. Murphy, 'Book Review: Histories of the Hanged and Britain's Gulag', *History* 91/303 (2006), 427–428

180. J. Newsinger, *British Counterinsurgency from Palestine to Northern Ireland* (Basingstoke, 2002)

181. J. Newsinger, 'Minimum Force, British Counter-Insurgency and the Mau Mau Rebellion', *Small Wars and Insurgencies* 3/1 (1992), 47–57

182. R. Thornton, '"Minimum Force": A Reply to Huw Bennett', *Small Wars and Insurgencies* 20/1 (2009), 215–226

Propaganda and Intelligence

183. R. Aldrich, *GCHQ: The Uncensored Story of Britain's Most Secret Intelligence Agency* (London, 2010)
184. R. Aldrich, 'Persuasion? British Intelligence, the History Policeman and Official Information' in P. Major and C. R. Moran (eds.), *Spooked: Britain, Empire and Intelligence Since 1945* (Newcastle, 2009), 29–50
185. C. Andrew, *Defence of the Realm: The Authorised History of MI5* (London, 2009)
186. S. Bhattacharya, *Propaganda and Information in Eastern India 1939–1945: A Necessary Weapon of War* (Richmond, 2001)
187. S. Carruthers, *Winning Hearts and Minds: British Governments, the Media and Colonial Counter-Insurgency 1944–1960* (London, 1995)
188. R. Cormac, *Confronting the Colonies: British Intelligence and Counterinsurgency* (London, 2013)
189. R. Cormac, 'Coordinating Covert Action: The Case of the Yemen Civil War and the South Arabian Insurgency', *Journal of Strategic Studies* 36/5, 692–717
190. M. Curtis, *Web of Deceit: Britain's Real Role in the World* (London, 2003)
191. P. Dimitrakis, 'British Intelligence and the Cyprus Insurgency', *Journal of Intelligence and Counterintelligence* 21/2 (2008), 375–394
192. S. Dorril, *MI6: Fifty Years of Special Operations* (London, 2000)
193. R. Drayton, 'Anglo-American "Liberal" Imperialism, British Guiana 1953–1964 and the World Since September 11' in Wm. R. Louis (ed.), *Yet More Adventures with Britannia* (London, 2005), 321–342
194. D. Easter, '"Keep the Indonesian Pot Boiling": Western Covert Intervention in Indonesia', *Cold War History* 5/1 (2005), 55–73
195. D. Easter, 'British Intelligence and Propaganda during the Confrontation 1963–1966', *Intelligence and National Security* 16/2 (2001), 83–102
196. C. Hashimoto, 'Fighting the Cold War or Post-Colonialism: Britain in the Middle East from 1948 to 1958', *International History Review* 36/1 (2014), 19–44
197. K. Jeffery, *MI6: The History of Secret Intelligence 1909–1949* (London, 2010)
198. C. Jones, '"Where the State Feared to Tread': Britain, Britons, Covert Action and the Yemen Civil War 1962–1964', *Intelligence and National Security* 21/5 (2006), 717–737
199. G. Kennedy and C. Tuck, 'Introduction' in G. Kennedy and C. Tuck, (eds.), *British Propaganda and Wars of Empire* (Farnham, 2014), 1–12
200. S. Mawby, 'The Clandestine Defence of Empire: British Special Operations in Yemen 1951–1964', *Intelligence and National Security* 17/3 (2002), 105–130
201. S. Mawby, 'Mr. Smith Goes to Vienna: Britain's Cold War in the Caribbean 1951–1954', *Cold War History* 13/4 (2013), 541–561

Bibliography

202. K. Morris, *British Techniques of Public Relations and Propaganda for Mobilizing East and Central Africa During World War II* (Lewiston, 2000), 103
203. P. Murphy, 'Intelligence and Decolonization: The Life and Death of the Federal Intelligence and Security Bureau', *Journal of Imperial and Commonwealth History* 29/2 (2001), 101–130
204. S. Rabe, *US Intervention in British Guiana: A Cold War Story* (Chapel Hill, 2005)
205. P. Satia, *Spies in Arabia: The Great War and the Cultural Foundations of Britain's Covert Empire in the Middle East* (Oxford, 2008)
206. M. Thomas, *Empires of Intelligence: Security Services and Colonial Disorder after 1945* (Berkeley, 2008)
207. H. I. Tijani, 'Britain and the Foundation of Anti-Communist Policies in Nigeria 1945–1960', *African and Asian Studies* 8 (2009), 47–66
208. C. Tuck, '"Cut the Bonds Which Bind Our Hands:" Deniable Operations During the Confrontation with Indonesia 1963–1966', *Journal of Military History* 77/2 (2013), 599–623
209. C. Tuck, 'British Propaganda and Information Operations against Indonesia 1963–1966' in G. Kennedy and C. Tuck (eds.), *British Propaganda and Wars of Empire* (Farnham, 2014), 145–168
210. C. Walton, *Empire of Secrets: British Intelligence, the Cold War and the Twilight of Empire* (London, 2013)
211. C. Walton and C. Andrew, 'Still the Missing Dimension: British Intelligence and the Historiography of British Decolonisation' in Patrick Major and Christopher R. Moran (eds.), *Spooked: Britain, Empire and Intelligence Since 1945* (Newcastle, 2009), 73–96
212. R. Waters and G. Daniels, 'The World's Longest General Strike: The AFL-CIO, the CIA and British Guiana', *Diplomatic History* 29/2 (2005), 279–307

Capital

213. S. Akita, G. Krozewski and S. Watanabe (eds.), *The Transformation of the International Order in Asia: Decolonization, the Cold War and the Colombo Plan* (Abingdon, 2015)
214. S. Akita (ed.), *Gentlemanly Capitalism, Imperialism and Global History* (Basingstoke, 2002)
215. L. J. Butler, *Copper Empire: Mining and the Colonial State in Northern Rhodesia 1930–1964* (Basingstoke, 2007)
216. P. J. Cain and A. G. Hopkins, *British Imperialism: Innovation and Expansion 1688–1914* (London, 1993)
217. P. J. Cain and A. G. Hopkins, *British Imperialism: Crisis and Deconstruction 1914–1990* (London, 1993)
218. P. J. Cain and A. G. Hopkins, 'Afterword: The Theory and Practice of British Imperialism' in R. E. Dumett (ed.), *Gentlemanly Capitalism and British Imperialism: The New Debate on Empire* (Harlow, 1999), 196–220

219. P. J. Cain and A. G. Hopkins, 'The Political Economy of British Expansion Overseas', *Economic History Review* 33/4 (1980), 463–490
220. R. E. Dumett (ed.), *Gentlemanly Capitalism and British Imperialism: The New Debate on Empire* (Harlow, 1999)
221. S. Galpern, *Money, Oil and Empire in the Middle East: Sterling and Post-war Imperialism* (Cambridge, 2009)
222. M. Havinden and D. Meredith, *Colonialism and Development: Britain and its Tropical Colonies* (London, 1993)
223. A. Hinds, *Britain's Sterling Colonial Policy and Decolonization* (London, 2001)
224. G. Krozewski, *Money and the End of Empire: British International Economic Policy and the Colonies 1947–1958* (Basingstoke, 2001)
225. G. Krozewski, 'Gentlemanly Imperialism and the British Empire after 1945' in S. Akita (ed.), *Gentlemanly Capitalism, Imperialism and Global History* (Basingstoke, 2002), 83–100
226. G. Krozewski, 'Finance and Empire: The Dilemma Facing Great Britain in the 1950s', *International History Review* 18/1 (1996), 48–69
227. M. Misra, *Business, Race and Politics in British India* (Oxford, 1999)
228. M. Misra, 'Gentlemanly Capitalism and the Raj: British Policy in India between the World Wars' in R. E. Dumett (ed.), *Gentlemanly Capitalism and British Imperialism: The New Debate on Empire* (Harlow, 1999), 157–174
229. I. Phimister, 'Corporate Profit and Race in Central African Copper Mining 1946–1958', *Business History Review* 85 (2011), 749–774
230. S. Stockwell, *The Business of Decolonization* (Oxford, 2000)
231. S. Stockwell, 'African Prospects: Mining the Empire for Britain in the 1950s' in M. Lynn (ed.), *The British Empire in the 1950s: Retreat or Revival* (Basingstoke, 2006), 77–99
232. R. L. Tignor, *Capitalism and Nationalism at the End of Empire* (Princeton, 1998)
233. N. White, *Business, Government and the End of Empire: Malaya 1942–1957* (Oxford, 1996)
234. N. White, 'Gentemanly Capitalism and Empire in the Twentieth Century: The Forgotten Case of Malaya 1914–1965' in R. E. Dumett (ed.), *Gentlemanly Capitalism and British Imperialism: The New Debate on Empire* (Harlow, 1999), 175–195
235. N. White, 'The Business and Politics of Decolonization: The British Experience in the Twentieth Century', *Economic History Review* 53/3 (2000), 544–564

Labour

236. K. O. Akurang-Parry, '"The Loads are Heavier than Usual": Forced Labor by Women and Children in the Central Province, Gold Coast', *African Economic History* 30 (2002), 31–51

237. K. O. Akurang-Parry, 'Transformations in the Feminization of Unfree Domestic Labor', *International Labor and Working Class History* 78 (2010), 28–47

238. N. Bolland, *The Politics of Labour in the British Caribbean* (Kingston, 2001)

239. A. Carew, 'The Trade Union Congress in the International Labour Movement' in A. Campbell, N. Fishman and J. McIroy (eds.), *British Trade Unions and Industrial Politics: The Post-War Compromise 1945– 1964* (Aldershot, 1999), 145–167

240. A. Carew, 'Conflict Within the ICFTU: Anti-Colonialism and Anti-Communism in the 1950s', *International Review of Social History* 41/2 (1996), 147–181

241. F. Cooper, *Decolonization and African Society: The Labor Question in French and British Africa* (Cambridge, 1996)

242. G. Curless, 'The Sudan is "Not Yet Ready for Trade Unions": The Railway Strikes of 1947–1948', *Journal of Imperial and Commonwealth History* 41/5 (2013), 804–822

243. M. Davis, 'Labour, Race and Empire: The TUC and Colonial Policy' in Billy Frank, Craig Horner and David Stewart (eds.), *The British Labour Movement and Imperialism* (Newcastle, 2010), 89–106

244. K. Grant, *A Civilized Savagery* (London, 2005)

245. K. Grant, 'Human Rights and Sovereign Abolitions of Slavery c. 1885–1956' in *Beyond Sovereignty: Britain, Empire and Transnationalism c. 1880–1950* (Basingstoke, 2007)

246. B. Grier, 'Pawns, Porters and Petty Traders: Women in the Transition to Cash Crop Agriculture in Colonial Ghana', *Signs* 17/2 (1992), 304–328

247. B. Grier, *Invisible Hands* (Portsmouth, NH, 2005)

248. D. Hyde, 'Undercurrents to Independence: Plantation Struggles in Kenya's Central Province 1959–1960', *Journal of Eastern African Studies* 4/3 (2010), 467–489

249. S. R. J. Long, 'Mixed Up in Power Politics and the Cold War: The Americans, the ICFTU and Singapore's Labour Movement 1955– 1960', *Journal of Southeast Asian Studies* 40/2 (2009), 323–352

250. P. E. Lovejoy, *Transformations in Slavery: A History of Slavery in Africa* (Cambridge, 1983)

251. S. Miers, *Slavery in the Twentieth Century* (Oxford, 2002)

252. M. Nicolson, *The TUC Overseas: The Roots of Policy* (London, 1986)

253. O. Okia, *Communal Labor in Colonial Kenya* (Basingstoke, 2012)

254. Y. Richards, *Maida Springer: Pan-Africanist and International Labor Leader* (Pittsburg, 2000)

255. S. Sen, 'Gender and Class: Women in Indian Industry 1890–1990', *Modern Asian Studies* 42/1 (2008), 75–116

256. M. Thomas, *Violence and Colonial Order: Police, Workers and Protest in the European Colonial Empires 1918–1940* (Cambridge, 2012)

257. L. White, 'Cars Out of Place: Vampires, Technology and Labor in East and Central Africa', *Representations* 43 (1993), 27–50

Notes

Chapter 1: Anti-Colonialism in the British Empire

1 Chin Peng, *Alias Chin Peng: My Side of History* (Singapore, 2003), 200.
2 GandhiServe Foundation, Collected Works, http://www.gandhiserve. org/e/cwmg/cwmg.htm.
3 Federal Archives Centre, University of the West Indies, Cave Hill, Barbados, FWI-GG-GA-44, Record of the 8th meeting of the West Indies Constitutional Conference, 8 January 1961.
4 E. Williams, *Inward Hunger* (Princeton, 2006), 45–47.
5 K. Nkrumah, *Consciencism* (London, 1964), 109.

Chapter 2: Britain and Britishness

1 S. Winder, 'À la recherché du Doctor Who', *The Guardian*, Review, 2 November 2013.
2 Churchill Archives Centre [CAC]: University of Cambridge, Sandys Papers, DSND 14/25, Box 2, Second Draft of Biggs-Davison Speech.
3 *The Times*, 16 January 1967, Marchers Surge on Downing Street, 1.
4 Churchill Archives Centre, Hailes Papers, HAIS 4/11, 'What I Said at Cabinet', 17 December 1956.
5 J. Stuart, *Within the Fringe* (London, 1967).
6 The National Archives [TNA]: CAB 195/15, CM(80)56, 6 November 1956, CM(89)56, 27 November 1956.
7 School of Oriental and African Studies, Movement for Colonial Freedom, Boxes 68–71.

Chapter 3: Migration

1 TNA: PREM 15/1258, Chief Whip's Office to Yonge, 8 August 1972, PREM 15/1259, Number 10 Duty Clerk to Roberts, 2 September 1972; PREM 15/1260, Heath minute on Kampala to FCO, 14 September 1972.

2 TNA: CAB 195/14, CM(39)55, 3 November 1955.
3 TNA: FCO 141/1428, Secretary of State to Governor (Seychelles), 13 November 1965.

Chapter 4: Counterinsurgency, Intelligence and Propaganda

1 India Office Records, British Library [IOR]: R/20/D/158, Chaplin to Commander FRA, 15 March 1965, including Political Directive for Operation Park (Annex A).
2 TNA: KV 2/3622, T/C on MCF (o/g) to Fenner from Peggy Rushton, 11 June 1957.

Chapter 5: Capital and Labour

1 Y. Richards, *Conversations with Maida Springer* (University of Pittsburgh, 2004), 185.
2 IOR: R/20/B/3035, Note of a Meeting on 20 August 1960.

Index